COURAGE TO REMEMBER

INTERVIEWS ON THE HOLOCAUST

OTHER PARAGON BOOKS ON THE HOLOCAUST

Holocaust: Religious and Philosophical Implications
Edited by John K. Roth and Michael Berenbaum, 1989

Different Voices: Women and the Holocaust
Edited by Carol Rittner and John K. Roth, 1993

Against All Hope: Resistance in the Nazi Concentration
Camps 1938-1945
By Herman Langbein, Edited by Harry Zohn, 1994

The Road to Hell: Recollection of the Nazi Death March
Written by Joseph Freeman and Edited by Donald Schrartz, 1998

COURAGE TO REMEMBER

INTERVIEWS ON THE HOLOCAUST

by

Kinue Tokudome

PARAGON HOUSE
St. Paul, Minnesota

Published in the United States of America by

Paragon House
2700 University Avenue West
St. Paul, Minnesota 55114

Library of Congress Catalog-in-Publication Data

Tokudome, Kinue. 1951—
      Courage to remember: interviews on the holocaust
            p.   cm.
      ISBN 1-55778-765-4 (cloth). — ISBN 1-55778-773-5 (paper)
      1. Holocaust, Jewish (1939-1945)—Influence. 2. Holocaust, Jewish (1939-1945)—
Personal narratives. 3. World War, 1939-1945—Jews-Rescue. 4. Righteous Gentiles in
the Holocaust. 5. Antisemitism—Japan—History.   I. Title
      D804.195.T64 1999
      940.53'18—dc21
                                                                98-42720
                                                                     CIP

10 9 8 7 6 5 4 3 2

CONTENTS

Acknowledgments

This book project was born out of a friendship, sustained by that friendship and dedicated to a friendship. It was the friendship between Japanese people and Jewish people—a friendship long overdue. Rabbi Abraham Cooper of the Simon Wiesenthal Center said to me when we first met that the best way to get rid of a stereotype one might have on any group of people would be to have a friend among them and know him or her personally.

What I hoped for this book was that it would help Japanese readers relate to the feelings of those who dedicated themselves to making the world remember the Holocaust and the lessons it taught. I hoped that this book would help Japanese readers feel close to these people as their fellow human beings—their friends.

I am grateful to all the fourteen people I interviewed, who not only checked the content of each chapter in which they appeared but also gave me their kindest support and advice. Two people deserve my deepest appreciation. Rabbi Abraham Cooper was a constant source of encouragement from the beginning, when this project was just a vague idea, until the end when I finished writing the last chapter. Dr. Neil Sandberg of the Asia and Pacific Rim Institute of the American Jewish Committee also provided me with many valuable insights which I would otherwise have lacked.

Professor Akira Iriye of Harvard University found more profound meaning than I had ever imagined for this book. I am grateful that he kindly wrote a foreword to the original Japanese edition. This English edition is also blessed with a fortune to have an introduction written by Dr. Richard L. Rubenstein, whose exchange with Elie Wiesel in 1970 on faith I read countless times with fascination. I am honored that he took the time to write a detailed background of the Japanese attitudes toward Jewish people so that American readers will better understand why I wrote this book. I would also like to thank Professor John K. Roth who encouraged me to publish this book in English.

My sincere appreciation also goes to Congressman Tom Lantos, Chicago Mercantile Exchange Chairman Emeritus Mr. Leo Melamed and Mr. Tachi Kiuchi of Mitsubishi Electric, each of whom wrote a generous recommendation for this book.

I would like to thank Dr. Alfred Balitzer of Claremont McKenna College and Mr. Yoshito Takigawa of the Israel Embassy in Tokyo for their kind advice.

My husband and my two teen-age children, my daughter and my son, deserve my gratitude for their never having lost a sense of humor while I was working on this project. For that I can only say, "Thank you."

Lastly I would like to dedicate this book to my parents in Sendai, Japan, my home town. This is a small way of showing my gratitude and respect for their courage to let their only daughter pursue her dream beyond their horizon when she was only eighteen.

Kinue Tokudome
Torrance, California
September, 1998

Introduction

Richard L. Rubenstein

Kinue Tokudome has produced a unique book concerning the ways
in which the Holocaust is remembered. A Japanese writer with advanced degrees in political science and international relations from
the University of Illinois at Chicago and the University of Chicago,
she has hitherto written primarily in Japanese about American issues
that in her opinion are not really understood by the Japanese people.
Among the least understood aspects of Western civilization in Japan
have been Judaism and the fate of the European Jews during World
War II. In *Courage to Remember* Ms. Tokudome seeks to set the record
straight.

Ms. Tokudome has been motivated in part to undertake this task
by the spate of anti-Semitic books and opinion articles that have in
recent years enjoyed an enormous publishing success in Japan, a country with no more than a few hundred permanent Jewish residents.
Masami Uno's *If You Understand the Jews, You Will Understand the
World* and *If You Understand the Jews, You Will Understand Japan*[1] has
been one of the more successful books of the genre. Uno takes up
two of the major themes of Japanese anti-Semitic literature, the myth
of a worldwide Jewish conspiracy to which Japan's major ill can be
ascribed and Holocaust denial. While denying that he is an anti-
Semite, Uno argues that the Holocaust is Jewish propaganda and
that Hitler and Stalin killed millions of Jews to protect their nations
from the Jewish threat. Not surprisingly, Uno quotes extensively from
the infamous forgery, *The Protocols of the Elders of Zion*.[2]

Nevertheless, in contrast to the spread of the anti-Semitic *literature*, there has been no history of continuous anti-Semitic *behavior*

in Japan. Even during World War II, Jews living in Japan were never threatened or treated with hostility as Jews.[3] Moreover, the Imperial Japanese government permitted the entry of almost 20,000 Jewish refugees into Shanghai and other Japanese-controlled territories in China. One of the most extraordinary Japanese rescue efforts on behalf of the Jews, that of Chiune Sugihara, Japanese Vice Consul in Kaunas, Lithuania in 1940, is discussed at length in *Courage to Remember*. Without official authorization but with considerable knowledge of the fate the Nazis had in store for the Jews, Sugihara issued transit visas that permitted as many as ten thousand Jews to escape across the Soviet Union to Japanese-held territory on the transparent pretext that they were travelling to Curacao in the Dutch West Indies. Without Sugihara, these Jews would almost certainly have perished in the Holocaust. Moreover, although Sugihara acted without consulting the Foreign Ministry, it nevertheless backed him up.[4]

When 2,000 of their number found themselves unable to proceed across the Pacific, Foreign Minister Yosuke Matsuoka issued orders extending their visas. In 1936 the same Matsuoka had committed Japan to the Tripartite Pact with Nazi Germany and Fascist Italy. When Matsuoka ordered the visas extended, no allied government was willing to take such a step. When the extensions finally ran out, the displaced Jews were sent to Shanghai where a total of about 17,000 Jews found themselves under Japanese protection in spite of insistent German attempts to pressure Japanese to exterminate them.

The Japanese first became aware of modern Jews as a distinct community as a result of the Russo-Japanese War of 1904-05. Initially, Japan was in danger of losing the war because of lack of funds. Baron Korekiyo Takahashi, Vice Governor of the Bank of Japan, was dispatched to London to negotiate emergency loans on the international markets, but found little interest among European bankers.[5] The Tsarist Empire was expected ultimately to wear Japan down. Finally, after weeks of negotiation Takahashi arrived at a provisional agreement with a banking consortium for a loan of £10,000,000, half to be issued immediately and half at a later date. Because it needed the entire sum immediately, the Japanese government was reluctant to accept.[6]

On April 4, 1904, Takahashi met the American-Jewish financier

Jacob Schiff at a London dinner party. Schiff was the head of Kuhn, Loeb and Company, then one of the two most powerful private investment banks in the United States, the other being J. P. Morgan. Takahashi was surprised to find Schiff "uncommonly interested in the war as well as in the affairs of Japan." The next day, a British banker informed Takahashi of Schiff's willingness to underwrite the additional £5,000,000 immediately. This was *before* Japan's first decisive victory in the battle of the Yalu River on May 1, 1904. Even more important to Takahashi was the fact that immediately after the loan was issued, King Edward VII gave a private lunch for Schiff and Sir Ernest Cassel, an English-Jewish banker of German origin and Schiff's partner in the venture. Cassel was Schiff's closest lifelong friend, both men having been born in Frankfurt.[7] Cassel was also an intimate of the king.[8] As Takahashi later learned, during the lunch the king expressed "his gracious appreciation" to Schiff for his part in the Japanese loan.

Takahashi was naturally interested in getting to know these two highly placed Jewish financiers of German origin. He discovered Schiff was not only strongly pro-Japanese but also "…justly indignant at the unfair treatment of the Jewish population by the Russian government."[9] Schiff was especially bitter about the Kishinev pogrom of April 6-7, 1903. He refused to permit Kuhn, Loeb to participate in underwriting any Imperial Russian loans and used his influence to prevent other firms from so doing.[10] According to Takahashi, Schiff was convinced that a government capable of such cruelties and outrages as the Imperial Russian government needed to be overhauled from its very foundations. Schiff saw the war loans to Japan as a step in that direction.

On November 14, 1904, the Japanese floated a further loan for £12,000,000, also at 6 percent. Again, Kuhn, Loeb underwrote half the issue. In addition to its material benefits, the loan proved a boost for Japanese morale at a critical moment. After the Russian forces at Port Arthur capitulated to the Japanese, a third loan was issued on March 28, 1905, for the sum of £30,000,000 at 4 1/2 percent. Again, Kuhn Loeb took half of the issue.

The first two loans had been issued by an Anglo-American consortium. A German syndicate led by M. M. Warburg and Company of Hamburg participated in the third. The Warburg bank was headed by Max M. Warburg. Relations between the Warburg bank and Kuhn, Loeb were exceptionally close. In 1875 Schiff married Therese Loeb, eldest daughter of Solomon Loeb, the firm's founder. In 1895 Paul M. Warburg (1868-1932), Max's brother, married Nina Loeb, another daughter of Solomon Loeb. In 1902 he moved to New York from Hamburg and became a Kuhn, Loeb partner. Paul's brother Felix (1871-1937) married Frieda Schiff, Jacob's daughter, in 1895. He too became a Kuhn Loeb partner. Max M. Warburg remained in Hamburg as the head of one of Germany's leading private banks.[11]

Max M. Warburg was the key person in securing German participation that included eleven German banks led by the Deutsch-Asiatische Bank. According to Takahashi, Schiff told him that he wanted German participation in order to avoid overloading the Anglo-American markets. Schiff also told Takahashi that he was prepared to proceed with the Germans as partner should the British decline to participate. *Thus, at a critical moment in modern Japanese history, Japan's first major war with a European power, an international consortium of Jewish bankers of German origin, closely related by marriage, provided the means to finance the war. More than any other, that event shaped the Japanese image of the Jew in the twentieth century.* Moreover, as noted, Takahashi clearly understood that Schiff's fundamental motive was anger at Tsarist Russia's treatment of the Jews and his desire to use his enormous financial power to bring about changes in Russian society. Takahashi also relates that, while the Germans were considering participation, Max M. Warburg and the president of the Deutsch-Asiatische Bank were invited to lunch by the Kaiser on his yacht and that the Kaiser urged them to proceed with the loan.

The role of Schiff and the other Jewish bankers in underwriting the loans left an indelible, albeit ironic, impression on the Japanese. Friendship between Schiff and Takahashi developed to such a point that the latter sent his daughter Wakiko to live with the Schiffs for three and a half years. As noted, Takahashi was greatly impressed by King Edward's luncheon with Schiff and Cassell and Kaiser Wilhelm's luncheon meeting with Max M. Warburg. As Tetsu Kohno writes,

> Japan won the war, acquired new territories and new resources, and its international prestige was enhanced. *As a result, the equa-*

tion of Jews with ownership of massive and global financial resources and thereby with the ability to manipulate world events, underlies until today nearly all debates on the Jewish question in Japan"(italics added).[12]

In the spring of 1906, Schiff visited Japan with his wife and a number of friends. The Emperor Meiji received him in private audience followed by a luncheon. On his arrival at the palace, Schiff was invested with the insignia of the Order of the Rising Sun, Japan's highest honor, and the Emperor thanked him for the important assistance rendered by him to the nation.[13] No other foreigner had ever been so honored by the Japanese.

Unfortunately, Schiff's financial support of Japan had dangerous unintended consequences. When *The Protocols of the Elders of Zion* was circulated in Japanese translation in the nineteen-twenties, Schiff's earlier activities on behalf of Japan enhanced their credibility. The *Protocols'* myth of a Jewish conspiracy to dominate the world first caught the attention of the Japanese military in the aftermath of the Russian Revolution. When the Bolsheviks attempted to control Eastern Siberia, the Japanese dispatched a 75,000 man expeditionary force to oppose them. The Japanese fought together with White Russian forces under the command of General Grigori Semyonov. The Bolsheviks defeated the White Russians and the Japanese whereupon General Semyonov ordered that each of his soldiers be given a copy of *The Protocols of the Elders of Zion*. Among the Japanese attached to the White Russians were Captain Norihiro Yasue, Naval Captain Koreshige Inuzuka, General Kiichiro Higuchi and General Nobutaka Shioden. All spoke Russian; all hated Bolshevism. *In the nineteen-thirties these were the men who were to take the lead in Japan's dealings with the Jews.* Unable to blame themselves for the defeat, the White Russians interpreted Bolshevism as the victory of a secret Jewish "government" over the Christian world.[14] To explain their failure, they distributed *The Protocols of the Elders of Zion* and other anti-Semitic literature throughout Europe and Asia. Japanese officers were especially susceptible to White Russian propaganda that offered a convenient rationalization of their own Siberian defeat. Schiff was also falsely accused by the White Russians and the Nazis of financing the Russian Revolution and came to be seen as the leader of the alleged

Jewish world conspiracy.[15] Though false, many Japanese found the accusation credible because of Schiff's known hostility to the Tsarist regime.

Japanese ultra-nationalists saw the Russian Revolution as proof of the alleged Jewish conspiracy. Three ancient dynasties, the Hohenzollern, the Hapsburg and the Romanov, had fallen. The Tsar and his family had been murdered. Given their reverence for the Emperor, the Japanese were deeply shocked. The ultra-nationalists held England and the United States responsible for much of the disorder. These nations, they claimed, had been Judaized. As did Uno in the nineteen-eighties, the ultras regarded Japan as the last bulwark against an alleged Jewish world conspiracy. The ultra-nationalists complained that Japanese culture was being polluted by the three S's, Screen, Sex, and Sport. Modernization, irreverence toward the Emperor, Marxism and Hollywood were all seen as Jewish tools to undermine traditional Japanese culture. Just as Uno saw the alleged Jewish control of the western media as an assault on Japan, so too did his nationalist predecessors in the twenties and thirties. Today much of Hollywood is owned by Japanese corporations such as Sony and Matsushita.

Ironically, while Japanese ultra-nationalists were as convinced as the Nazis during the thirties and even later that there was a Jewish world conspiracy, they reacted very differently than did the Nazis. In a January 18, 1939, report to the Imperial Naval General Staff, Naval Captain Koreshige Inuzuka spelled out the difference:

> [The Jews are] just like a *fugu* (blowfish) dish. It is very delicious but unless one knows well how to cook it, it may prove fatal to his life.[16]

The "experts" were convinced that they knew how to prepare this particular *fugu*. Precisely because they were regarded as dangerous, most, but not all, influential Japanese anti-Semites were convinced that the Jews had to be handled with special care. Nevertheless, they rejected Nazi demands that they cooperate in the so-called "Final Solution."

As Japan's relationship with Nazi Germany strengthened, Japanese authorities decided to formulate a Jewish policy. In December 1938 the Imperial Japanese government declared that Jews would be treated no differently than any other foreigners, a policy wholly at odds with Germany's. The policy facilitated the entry of thousands of Jews into Japanese-occupied Shanghai, including the students and rabbis of the Mir Yeshiva, one of the world's most important institutions of rabbinic higher learning and one of the few such institutions whose personnel largely survived the Holocaust. Armed with transit visas issued by Vice Consul Chiune Sugihara in Kovno, most of the yeshiva's students and rabbis eventually made their way to Shanghai.

The story of Shanghai as a refuge has been told elsewhere.[17] Here we note that the refugees survived the war under official programs formulated by leading Japanese anti-Semites. Some Japanese anti-Semites wanted to follow the lead of the Nazis all the way, but that policy did not win the day. The *fugu* plan itself did not survive the attack on Pearl Harbor. During the war the borders of the Japanese empire were closed to new Jewish immigration, and the conditions of the Jews of Shanghai grew progressively worse. Nevertheless, no amount of Nazi pressure was able to alter the Japanese determination not to submit to German demands that they exterminate the Jews within their territories.

After the war, the Japanese people were shocked when they learned of the Nazi death camps and the behavior of their former German ally. Nevertheless, the anti-Jewish literature of the Nazi period survived and was never subject to critical scrutiny as it was in West Germany. This made the Japanese all the more susceptible to a revival of anti-Semitic literature and mendacious attempts to deny the Holocaust on the part of those who would gladly repeat the slaughter if they could.

Ms. Tokudome is acutely sensitive to those trends. She describes an encounter with Renee Firestone, a survivor of the "death marches," one of the most vicious Nazi assaults, in which she expresses shame for the fact that many anti-Semitic books and books denying the Holocaust have been published in her native land.[18] In response Ms. Firestone tells her to think about what she can do rather than being ashamed of the lies of others. *Courage to Remember* is Ms. Tokudome's attempt to set the record straight. In pursuit of that objective, she has interviewed survivors, the children of survivors, historians, theologians and clergymen. In addition to Ms. Firestone, these include Miles

Lerman, Michael Berenbaum, Simon Wiesenthal, Peter Willnauer of Austria, Raul Hilberg, Neil C. Sandberg, Annette Lantos, Leo Melamed, Hillel Levine, David A. Harris, Abraham Cooper, Makoto Otsuka, and John K. Roth. The common thread uniting all of the respondents is their passionate commitment to keeping the memory of the Holocaust alive as those who lived through the events pass away and the temptation to falsify memory by the political and spiritual heirs of the perpetrators intensifies.

The memory they seek to perpetuate is not only that of the evil inflicted upon defenseless victims. It is also the memory of the morally significant but numerically sparse instances of what Hillel Levine has identified as a "conspiracy of goodness." The memory of two extraordinary examples of a "conspiracy of goodness" pervades much of this work, the audacious rescue efforts of two non-Jews, Chiune Sugihara and Raoul Wallenberg. Ms. Tokudome includes a meditation on one of the most extraordinary Japanese efforts on behalf of the Jews in the form of a "letter" from Boston University Professor Hillel Levine, author of the most comprehensive and authoritative attempt to understand Chiune Sugihara, to the now deceased Sugihara. She also shares with us some of her correspondence and conversation with Leo Melamed, Chairman Emeritus and Senior Policy Advisor of the Chicago Mercantile Exchange, who owes his life to the transit visa Sugihara issued to his family when he was a boy of eight. In a similar vein, Annette Lantos, also a survivor and wife of California congressman Tom Lantos, remembers how they and thousands of other Hungarian Jews were saved by the heroic efforts of Swedish diplomat Raoul Wallenberg in Nazi-occupied Budapest. Sugihara and Wallenberg used their diplomatic posts to issue life-saving paper to tens of thousands who would otherwise have perished at a time when the paper of the Nazi bureaucracy had the power to kill. When Soviet forces occupied Budapest, they imprisoned Wallenberg, who later died in a Russian prison. Mrs. Lantos tells the story of Wallenberg's heroism and of her husband's efforts to pierce the almost impenetrable wall of secrecy used by Soviet authorities to hide Wallenberg's fate. Miles Lerman, Chairman of the United States Holocaust Memorial Council, has a very different story to tell. He escaped from a German slave labor camp and formed a Jewish resistance group of 350 young men and women. Against all odds, Lerman's group fought the Germans for 23 months. When he returned to his native town after the war, he found only eleven Jews alive in a town with 16,000 Jewish inhabitants before the war.

A different story is told by Michael Berenbaum, born in the United States in 1945 and currently President and CEO of the Survivors of the Shoah Visual History Foundation. The Foundation is dedicated to preserving the memory of the Holocaust by gathering the testimony of 50,000 Holocaust survivors with the aid of the most advanced multi-media technology. This is perhaps the most graphic means of preserving memory for generations yet to come. Together with the supporting material that gives the personal accounts a larger social context, the testimonies will serve as a teaching resource par excellence.

In addition, more than any other individual Berenbaum is responsible for the distinctive planning that gave the US Holocaust Memorial Museum its universal appeal. Berenbaum understood that the Holocaust museum—located in close proximity to the national capital's shrines, museums and historic monuments—had to relate meaningfully to the larger American society rather than primarily to the religious group most directly affected by it. By common agreement, Berenbaum's efforts to "Americanize" the Holocaust have been extraordinarily successful. The vast majority of those visiting the Museum are non-Jews from the United States and elsewhere in the world.

In discussing the "Americanization" of the Holocaust with Berenbaum, Ms. Tokudome asks whether there can be a "Japanization" of the Holocaust. Berenbaum answers affirmatively. Recognizing that the Holocaust means "a little bit less" to the Japanese than to Europeans and Americans, Berenbaum quite rightly affirms that the Holocaust can have a distinctive meaning for the Japanese. He tells Ms. Tokudome that one of the issues raised by the Holocaust is "the limit of universal responsibility," always a potential problem, especially in relatively homogeneous communities like Japan. He states that the difference between rescuers like Wallenberg and Sugihara and the perpetrators was that "the rescuers regarded the Jews as human beings just like they were." Although simple, the observation is very much to the point.

As of this writing, Japan has been experiencing a prolonged recession bordering on a depression. As noted above, the myth of a worldwide Jewish conspiracy provides some influential groups within Japan with a convenient way to avoid responsibility for the mess and blame it on outsiders. Because the practical consequences of anti-Semitic canards have proven so inhumanly destructive, a further denial is attractive to these same groups, namely, denial that the Holocaust ever happened. Ms. Tokudome fully understands the potentially destructive consequences of both the myth of a Jewish conspiracy and Holocaust denial. Several of her respondents discuss current efforts to offer the Japanese accurate knowledge of Judaism and the Holocaust. Rabbi Abraham Cooper has been especially active in that endeavor, working primarily at the personal level, offering seminars in Japan, writing newspaper articles, in effect, building bridges to the Japanese.

Another of Ms. Tokudome's respondents, Rev. Makoto Otsuka, Director of the Holocaust Education Center of Japan located in Fukuyama, Hiroshima Prefecture, has been building bridges from the Japanese side. His interest in the Holocaust began when he met Otto Frank, father of Anne Frank, more than a quarter of a century ago and eventually resulted in a Holocaust memorial museum in Japan.

Ms. Tokudome's final respondent is Professor John K. Roth, the son of a Presbyterian minister and the author of many books on the Holocaust. A deeply committed Christian, Professor Roth first became interested in the Holocaust as a result of reading Elie Wiesel in 1972 about the time his daughter Sarah was born. Reading Wiesel convinced Roth that the Holocaust posed a profound challenge to Christianity. In over 20 books and hundreds of articles, including a book co-authored with this writer, Roth has explored Jewish-Christian relations, the theological implications of the Holocaust, and the challenges the Holocaust poses for both ethics and philosophy.

Roth is well acquainted with Japan, having served as a visiting professor at Doshisha University in Kyoto in 1981 and 1982. In her dialogue with Roth, Ms. Tokudome discusses the debate among the Japanese concerning how their history is to be taught. She points out that there are groups in Japan who argue that if there is too much emphasis on the dark side of Japanese history young people will not feel proud of their community. Having come to understand the role of Christianity in the Holocaust while remaining a faithful Christian, Roth counsels facing the truth about one's own history, criticizing those aspects that deserve criticism and affirming what is of value. Roth rejects denial and the falsification of memory and history. When asked whether accepting the dark side of his own tradition's history has caused him to lose faith and commitment, he can honestly say no. He can also counsel the same combination of honesty and affirmation for others. And, it is precisely those virtues that Ms. Tokudome is trying to instil in her own people.

NOTES

[1]Both books are published by Tokuma Shoten, Tokyo, 1986.

[2]I am indebted to David Goodman, "Japanese Anti-Semitism," *The World and I*, November 1987, p. 401.*op. cit.,* for this summary of Uno's ideas. For a more comprehensive view, see David Goodman and Miyazawa Mazanori, *Jews in the Japanese Mind: The History and Uses of a Cultural Stereotype* (New York: The Free Press, 1994).

[3]In a speech delivered at the Symposium on "Japan and the Jews: Past Present and Future" held at the Japan Society of New York on April 10-11, 1989, Mr. Isaac Shapiro, a distinguished lawyer and past president of the Japan Society, recalled growing up in wartime Japan. He reported that he had never experienced anti-Semitism there although he was obviously regarded by his peers as a *gaijin,* a foreigner. Shapiro was born of Russian-Jewish parents in 1931 and speaks Japanese. His father has confirmed his experience. Insofar as the elder Shapiro experienced anti-Semitism in wartime Japan, it was from the foreign community not the Japanese.

[4]On Sugihara, see Hillel Levine's ground-breaking study, *In Search of Sugihara* (New York: The Free Press, 1996).

[5]Takahashi later served as Prime Minister. He was assassinated during the February 26, 1936 uprising by extremist army officers while again serving as Finance Minister

[6]This account of Takahashi's relations with Jacob Schiff is derived prima-

rily from Takahashi's memorandum on the subject. The English translation is found in Cyrus Adler, *Jacob H. Schiff: His Life and Letters* (Garden City: Doubleday, Doran, 1929), Vol. I, 213-30.

[7]Adler, *op. cit.,* Vol. II, 327.

[8]King Edward was so devoted to Cassel that he insisted on seeing him on the last day of his life, May 6, 1910. The meeting was scheduled for 11:00 AM. However, Cassel was told not to come because the king was too weak. When Cassel did not arrive, the king sent a second message asking Cassel to come immediately which he did. Adler, *op. cit.,* Vol. II, 328-29.

[9]Adler, *op. cit.,* 217.

[10]Article "Schiff, Jacob Henry" in *Encyclopaedia Judaica* (Jerusalem: Keter Publishing House, 1972), Vol. 14, 961.

[11]For an excellent history of the Warburg family, see Ron Chernow, *The Warburgs* (New York: Random House, 1993).

[12]Tetsu Kohno, "The Jewish Question in Japan, "The Jewish Question in Japan," in *The Jewish Journal of Sociology,* Vol. XXIX, No. 1, June 1987, 39-40.

[13]Adler, *op. cit.,* 227-28.

[14]Kohno, *op. cit.,* 40.

[15]Norman Cohn, *Warrant for Genocide* (New York: Harper and Row, 1967), 126.

[16]Cited by David Kranzler, *Japanese, Nazis and Jews: The Jewish Refugee Community of Shanghai, 1935-1945* (Hoboken: KTAV, 1988), 169.

[17]Kranzler, *op. cit.,* is the most comprehensive source.

[18]As the war was coming to an end, Germans forced tens of thousands of weakened, famished, poorly clad Jews out of camps such as Auschwitz and compelled them to march hundreds of miles towards camps in Germany. Those who could not continue were either shot on the spot or left to die.

We Are Much Stronger Than We Think We Are

Renee Firestone
Auschwitz Survivor, Holocaust Lecturer

I first saw Renee Firestone, an Auschwitz survivor, when I was in a small audience at the Museum of Tolerance in Los Angeles listening to her testimony. Everything about her—the way she talked, smiled and related to the audience, especially to young people—touched me in such a way that it was hard to describe except to say, "She is a beautiful person."

I went back to the Museum many times just to listen to her testimony and to observe the reactions of a young audience which was often as moving as her story itself. Once, she was talking to a roomful of high school students, describing how she, her sister and her parents were deported to Auschwitz in a cattle car. She said that there was no food or water for three days for more than a hundred people who were crammed into that tiny cattle car. The young audience listened attentively, and tears came to the eyes of many when she said, "When we were herded into the cattle car I was wearing a bathing suit under my regular clothes. My father had bought me that beautiful floral bathing suit before the Nazis occupied Hungary and it symbolized the happy and carefree days that I had enjoyed. I wanted to bring something with me that would remind me of all the wonderful memories." She was 19. Her mother was immediately sent to the gas chamber upon their arrival at Auschwitz and her sister five months later. She also lost her father a few months after the war.

Her soft voice filled the room, "I know that no person could ever understand what happened during the Holocaust. But I want to at least open up your hearts and let you be reminded that unless we are tolerant of one another, a similar tragedy can happen again. I'd like you to respect one another so that all the different people can enrich our lives."

After the testimony, many students went over to her and thanked her personally for sharing her story with them. I witnessed this warm exchange so many times and knew that it was very hard for the audience to leave the room without showing their deep appreciation for her. I felt the same way each time I sat in the audience.

Renee's family, like most other Hungarian Jews, was living in relative peace in Ungvar, Hungary, until March of 1944 when the Nazis finally occupied Hungary. The fate of the Hungarian Jews was particularly tragic in the history of the Holocaust because they were destroyed while the Germans were definitely losing the war. "...this last large and relatively intact community of nearly 800,000 Jews was subjected to the most ruthless, speedy, and concentrated destruction process of the war. Within a few months, all of the Jews in Hungary, with the exception of those in Budapest, were sent to concentration camps, mainly Auschwitz."[1]

Renee remembers how it happened to her family:

> Nearly 4000 Jews had been assembled in our ghetto, and approximately half of us would be leaving on the first transport. Guards started to load the trains at 10 o'clock on the morning of May 17 putting 100 to 120 people in each cattle car. It was a long process, the people moved slowly, and the Germans were careful not to harass anyone and cause a panic.
>
> At about five in the evening, the cars were closed and locked, as were the small barred windows located on the side of the car near the ceiling, so that we had very little light. Surely it was going to be a short trip, we thought. After all, we had no food or water, and there was but a single bucket in each car to serve as a toilet. We can't be going far...
>
> For three days and three nights we were packed in the cattle car. The stench of human waste became nauseating, and my throat and lips became parched from the lack of water. Not everyone in the car had a place to sit down, so most of us who were young and healthy tried to stand, allowing the older people and the babies to have the floor. Seldom did anyone speak. I do not remember participating in any conversations, except to lean down and whisper to my mother. She sat crying and moaning near my

feet, convinced that this was the end, that we would never see each other again. I kept telling her, "Everything will be all right." Somehow, I felt a spirit within me which did not permit me to develop a negative attitude...

"Raus!"(Out!) a guard shouted, as hundreds of us staggered from the train. Many of the older people, having been crowded into the cars like sardines, needed help simply to stand on their feet. Others, whom we now saw, had died during the journey. Their bodies were dumped onto the muddy ground. S.S. men were everywhere, some with rifles, some with growling German shepherd dogs on leashes. Up ahead, an S.S. officer, later identified as Dr. Mengele, the infamous "Angel of Death", separated us with a flick of his leather whip. "You go left, you go right."

We were led through a gate whose crest cynically bore the words "Arbeit Macht Frei," (work sets you free). We were then separated by sex, men going in one direction, women the other.

Hundreds of prisoners were housed in barracks, or "blocks" as they were called. A two foot high brick divider ran down the center of the building, and each side was lined with three tiered bunks. Ten or more people were expected to sleep shoulder-to-shoulder in every bunk, with a total of at least 1000 women sharing each barrack...

Death was all around us. It was hellish, not knowing whether this was to be my last day on earth. The chimneys were always smoking and the stench of burning flesh permeated the camp... My cousin Charlie's parents as well as my own mother, were killed moments after they disembarked from the train...and my dear sister, Klara, surviving only five months at Auschwitz, was also taken away and put to death.

Oddly enough, while in Auschwitz, my perspective and relative strengths seemed to change. Going in, I tended to be very skeptical about our odds for survival, but never willing to succumb or surrender. Then, in the face of so much danger, and death, I seemed to muster an inner strength and confidence that kept me going, because, somehow, I knew I was going to survive. I simply had to.

...Someone passed the word: "The Nazis are liquidating Auschwitz. The Russian are very close."...At the gate we were surrounded by S.S. soldiers armed with machine guns and German shepherd dogs. Our mournful journey began, one which later would become known as the "Death March."

Any woman falling behind, complaining, or simply losing her composure along the way was immediately shot. We lost close to a hundred women that first day. And so we walked, mile after mile after mile. Nobody spoke. Some were terrified; others seemed to have no feelings left at all.[2]

Renee was liberated by the Soviet army in May of 1945 at the Liebau concentration camp near the old Polish-Czechoslovakia border. Later she was reunited with her brother, Frank, but her father who was gravely ill with tuberculosis died a few months after the war. She got married to Bernard Firestone, a friend of her brother's, and in 1948 they emigrated to the United States with their baby daughter. She said, "Life was indeed starting all over for me. I launched a career as a fashion designer, and only on occasion paused to reflect on my earlier existence in Ungvar. My mother, father and Klara were always with me, not only in my values and moral, but in my work and in my heart. My memories would stay with me always."[3]

Renee's life as a successful fashion designer and lecturer of fashion art changed dramatically when she received a phone call from Rabbi Abraham Cooper of Simon Wiesenthal Center, a newly launched Jewish human rights organization in Los Angeles, in 1978. That same year, the American neo-Nazis marched in the town of Skokie, Illinois, while NBC aired a TV miniseries *The Holocaust* which introduced for the first time to millions of homes what happened in the Holocaust. Alarmed by the militant activities of the American neo-Nazi groups yet encouraged by people's newly awakened interest in the Holocaust, Rabbi Cooper thought that bringing together an individual who actually witnessed and experienced those events with young people was, from the educational point of view, the best thing to do.

Renee was to become a tireless volunteer for the Simon Wiesenthal Center's Educational Outreach Program. For the next twenty years she would lecture to more than a half million people, adults and students of all ages and walks of life, about her experiences as a Holocaust survivor. She has been interviewed countless times on television and by newspapers. Currently, she is also involved with the "Survivors of the Shoah Visual History Foundation," an organization created by Steven Spielberg for the purpose of recording oral testimony from survivors of the Holocaust.

I sat in her living room one day and listened to her as she reflected on her activities in the past twenty years.

How did it all begin ?

> When I received a phone call from Rabbi Cooper, I didn't know who he was. He somehow found out that I was a survivor. At that time I was teaching fashion design at UCLA, so he must have realized that probably I knew how to speak. He called me asking if I could come and tell my story. I thought it was ridiculous. I was quite successful in the fashion business and I really did not want to talk about that unique experience. I said to him that I really didn't know how much I remembered and that I had never thought about it or talked about it. Then he told me about a recent incident of a Jewish cemetery near Los Angeles being desecrated, swastikas sprayed all over the tombstones. I didn't want to believe it. I just couldn't believe that in the United States, something like this could happen after the Holocaust. So, I said to him that I really had to think about it and that I would call him back.
>
> That night, all night, I dreamt about the Holocaust. I was back in the camp. I had not had nightmares already for a long time. But I woke up to this nightmare screaming, "Never again! never again!" I asked myself, "What is this? what brought this on?" Then I thought, "Maybe we should start talking about it. Maybe we were silent for too long."

So it was not only you, but most of the survivors had never talked about their experiences up until that time?

> That's right. We would mention the Holocaust when we survivors get together and have foods on the table, like "Remember we used to say if we had only three potatoes every day we would be happy?" So there were these kinds of remarks, but we were never really talking about what happened.
>
> I called Rabbi Cooper and said to him, " I'll be honest with you. I don't know how much I remember, but I will come and tell whatever I remember." So we went to this temple where the

meeting would be held, but he didn't tell me that he's going to show a film called "Night and Fog." This was the very first documentary that was made about the Holocaust. It was not a good documentary, nevertheless it showed bodies being bulldozed into a mass grave. I was very affected by the film and started crying. I just couldn't stop. When the film was over and the lights went on, I was still sobbing. Rabbi Cooper came over to me and said, "Do you think you can say a few words?"

I got up and started to talk about Auschwitz. It was like I did not know where it came from. I just heard myself saying things that never went through my mind. It was just like coming from my guts. I kept thinking, "How come I remembered this. All these years I never remembered it...." And I talked, talked and talked. It was pouring out of me.

After it was over, people came over to me and showed this overwhelming outpouring of sympathy and love.

Were you surprised?

Very much so, because people were really not interested until then. When we came to this country, we needed to talk. That was when our memories were fresh and we needed to tell the people what had happened to us. But they used to say, "Oh, don't talk about it. Forget it. The war is over. Go on with your life." And it was like cutting us off again. It felt like, "They didn't listen then and they still don't want to hear it." It was very painful and that's why we stopped talking.

So this was an eye opener to me to see the people who were really interested and asking questions. Since then, two of us, Rabbi Cooper and I, were the outreach program of the Simon Wiesenthal Center, traveling to schools and to churches. It was a very interesting time for both of us.

You seem to be interested particularly in reaching out to young people. Why?

I am optimistic about young people. They are very curious, they really want to know. They are also frightened. Young people today in the United States are scared. A lot of things are going on in the society which are frightening. Family units are not like they used to be. It's not like in Japan. They often have no place to turn for advice. So, when they hear me talk especially about what terrible things can happen if we don't care about other human beings and each other, they understand. They understand that through humanity, through changing humanity, things will be better for them in the future. They really want to believe that humanity is good. They just need to be assured that they can do a lot of good in the world. I always tell them that they have the power to change the world. Only they have the power to change the world.

I heard you talk about it many times and I think that is the most moving message you are sending to young audiences. Also, as I observe you and your young audience, I am always amazed by your ability to connect with young people, and by their affection toward you. Why do you think you can do that?

I give them hope. They see that somebody like me, who was about their age when it happened, in spite of all the evil around me, managed to survive, and when it was over I came back into this world and made something of myself. The hope is that if you are willing to do something for yourself and for others, you can accomplish whatever you want to accomplish. I believe that as long as somebody doesn't come to you and put a gun to your head and shoot you, you have this free will to make of yourself whatever you want if you are willing to work for it. I think seeing a living example like myself, that's what young people need. They need to know that there is something in the future, no matter how bad things may be today. There is a future if that's what you want.

This may be a simplistic question. But how was it possible that after everything you had gone through that you still retained your strength and humanity?

I personally believe, and that's another thing I tell them, that we are much stronger than we think we are. We all have strength and strength disappears only when you give up. The strengths are there. We all have more strengths than you can imagine. So, don't give up. Just don't give up. That's what happened to me in the camp. I could have just laid down and died like many who did. But I wasn't going to do that.

But you did not know that you had that strength in you.

No, that's why you cannot give up. You just have to believe in yourself and believe in whatever you call it, God or Nature. There is a higher power that will help you if you will help yourself.

Since I listened to your testimony many times I know every gathering with you is memorable, but do you remember any particular exchange with your audience that was really special?

Well, occasionally, I have children of German parents in the audience. They would come over to me and say, "I want you to know that my parents are German and my father was in the war." And I am always wondering, "What is this need for this child to come and tell me?" Because he is in the audience with Americans I would never know that this person is a son of German S.S. But, he has this need to come and tell me. It happens many times as if they need my forgiveness.

Also, I often have young students visiting from Germany in the audience. I would say to them, "This is what I learned from my own experience. I do not judge people collectively but I judge every human being on his own merit. How can I say that all Germans are bad." Usually, some of these kids would come to me and say how they appreciated that I had said that.

Other thing I do is to work with police departments with children who are arrested and incarcerated because of their racist activities.

Do you find it difficult to talk to these children?

No, it's not difficult at all because I just meet them as a human being. I just tell them my story, and tell them how I feel about human beings. And in many cases, I found that they understood. I always go into a group or into a class thinking that if I reach one person in a group, I accomplish what I came to do.

When I talk to children, I tell them that I am not there to change their minds or make up their minds, but to open their minds and to talk about something they otherwise wouldn't think about. It's up to them whether they want to follow up and read about it. Most of the time I get letters afterward from the children telling me that after listening to my story they went to a library to learn more about the Holocaust and so forth.

You are also very much involved in Steven Spielberg's "Survivors of the Shoah Visual History Foundation." Can you explain what do you do for them?

I interview Holocaust survivors. I find that survivors trust me because I am one of them.

But isn't it difficult for you to interview other survivors since, each time you listen to their stories, you must relive your own tragedy?

It is. But I realized how little I knew about the Holocaust. I was in it, but I didn't know how complex this was. Now, the more I know, the more I want to know. I am just driven by wanting to know more.

For yourself or for the future generation to know?

Of course I want all these testimonies to be recorded for future generations. But, it's also my curiosity to understand. Since I have been interviewing survivors, liberators and rescuers, I am beginning to realize how enormous the Holocaust was. I don't think that the story of the Holocaust will ever be told in its entirety. It's just impossible. There are so many different aspects of it.

How do they respond when you interview them? I imagine that for many of them it must be the first time that they speak about their experiences in a formal setting.

Many times, it isn't just the first time in a formal setting, it is the first time they talk about it in general. When I call a few days after the interview to follow up and ask how they feel, they would say, "I feel like a stone fell off my heart." So, most of the times, it is a good effect. They were glad that they unloaded finally what was on their chest.

I told Mr. Spielberg at a dinner party publicly, "All these years, we survivors kept asking ourselves why I survived and why my sister or cousin who were smarter and better looking did not. Why me? But after I have been doing this work that you mad possible for us, I feel that my survival was justified." Mr. Spielberg was very touched by my words.

I have been touched by the devotion of Holocaust survivors to their efforts in telling their experiences to the next generation, not just Jewish but all the young people, so they could learn the lessons from history. Unfortunately, the Japanese WWII generation on the whole, I think, are not telling what they went through during the war to the young Japanese people as honestly and forthcomingly as they could.

We take our life for granted and take our family for granted. We feel that we don't have to talk about it. Holocaust survivors didn't think about it either twenty years ago. But now we feel that we must tell our children and grandchildren our unique experiences because they are the ones who will live in the legacy of these events.

Most of the time, history has been written by historians throughout generations. That's why "Survivors of the Shoah project" is so unique. Thanks to Mr. Spielberg, we are documenting the history through the people who actually experienced it.

If the older generation in Japan are not talking to their children and grandchildren about their experiences, you have to cultivate the environment where they can talk.

As I learned more about the Holocaust, especially the unbearable living conditions of the Auschwitz camps, my admiration for Renee grew. Occasionally, however, I had to ask myself if I really understood her sufferings. How many times did I encounter the expression "You will never understand unless you were there." while reading books about the Holocaust? A famous Holocaust literature critic, Lawrence L. Langer wrote about the struggle of Holocaust survivors:

The seeds of anguished memory are sown in the barren belief

that the very story you try to tell drives off the audience you seek to capture. Those seeds often shrivel in the further suspicion that the story you tell *cannot* be precisely the story as it happened. Reluctance to speak has little to do with *preference* for silence." [4]

It was usually after reading such passage that I paused and had a flash of doubt that I would ever be able to write about her. At other times, I read the essay Renee wrote about her trip to Auschwitz for the 50th anniversary of its liberation and couldn't stop crying:

As we neared Auschwitz-Birkenau, my heart began to race. As soon as I stepped out of the van I knew I must go through with it. When I stepped off the ramp and took a few steps on the railroad tracks, through my mind's eye I saw Mengele standing there and empty ramp filled with people spilling out of the cattle cars. I saw my mother going to the left, while my sister Klara and I went to the right. Where is dad? Why does it feel as if it happened yesterday?

We went to the C. Lager, to my barrack (number 28) where Klara and I slept on the same bunk, wrapped in each other's arms.... Next, we went through the bath house where my beautiful blond hair had been shaved and I was shrouded in a garment which was probably stripped from bodies gassed and cremated before us.

It wasn't until we walked to the ruins of Crematorium 5 that I panicked. A feeling that I would never find my way out of here overwhelmed me. It was here that my mother was gassed and probably Klara also. I lit a candle and said Kaddish...The crowd silently dispersed and I gave thanks to G-d that we could walk out the gate leaving no one behind, and that we didn't ever have to come back again....[5]

Then I remember my conversation with Rabbi Abraham Cooper who has observed Renee addressing young people hundreds of times. He told me, "What Renee does is an act of loving kindness. If there was ever a generation that had a right to reject hope and love, it would be the survivors of these horrible events. Yet, she made a choice that enriched all of our lives. Young people in the United States today learn so much about things but they don't have too many personal connections to anything. Adults very often don't have the time or take the time to share what they really think or what they really feel. For a person like Renee to simply take the time to be available for young people, that's a very powerful connection. I was also very much aware from the very first program that each speech comes with a great price. Going back and reliving those moments was a spiritually exhausting effort that, I think, took great courage. I am just grateful that she and other survivors have shown that kind of power, a moral power."

To me personally, Renee has been an inspiration. When I said to her that I was ashamed of the fact that many irresponsible anti-Semitic books, even ones denying the Holocaust, were sold in Japan, she said to me, "You don't have to be ashamed of what other Japanese do. You are only responsible for what you do or what you don't do. Think about what you can do." These words sustained me throughout the time I was writing this book. She told me that if she could reach one person at a time, her effort was worthwhile. I will always be grateful that she did not choose silence and that she tried to reach me.

NOTES

[1] Randolph L. Braham, "Hungarian Jews," in *Anatomy of the Auschwitz Death Camp* ed. Yisrael Guttman and Michael Berenbaum (Bloomington: Indiana University Press, 1994), 456.

[2] The Holocaust Remembrance Committee of Michael Diller High School, *Lest We Forget*, 1994. 32-48.

[3] Ibid

[4] Lawrence L. Langer, *Holocaust Testimonies: The Ruins of Memory* (New Haven : Yale University Press, 1991), 61.

[5] Renee Firestone, "A Personal Recollection," *Response*, The Simon Wiesenthal Center, Spring 1995.

Building a Temple of Memory and Learning

Miles Lerman, Chairman
The United States Holocaust Memorial Council

The United States Holocaust Memorial Museum is located adjacent to the National Mall in Washington, D.C., the center of American democracy today. Opened in 1993, this national institution teaches visitors the history of the Holocaust, and serves as America's memorial to the millions of people murdered during the Holocaust. Its mission statement defines the Holocaust as "the state-sponsored, systematic persecution and annihilation of European Jewry by Nazi Germany and its collaborators between 1933 and 1945."[1] It also teaches the visitors that millions of non-Jewish victims also perished in the Holocaust.

Its permanent exhibit starts on the fourth floor. On the way up there I was alone in the elevator watching an overhead monitor and listening to the voice of an American soldier who liberated a Nazi concentration camp. "Sick, dying, starved people...uh, such a sight as that, you...you can't imagine it. You, you just...things like that don't happen."

I knew it did happen and had a fair amount of knowledge of how it happened from my reading of Holocaust-related books and listening to survivors' testimonies. So, my visit to the Holocaust Museum was to confirm what I had already learned and to see firsthand its acclaimed exhibit. But, what a confirmation that was!

As I exited the elevator I encountered a large picture which showed the horrors of Ohrdruf slave-labor camp in Germany as seen by the American soldiers.

They were watching the charred corpses of inmates. I learned that General Eisenhower made a visit there "deliberately in order to

13

be in a position to give firsthand evidence of these things if ever, in the future, there develops a tendency to charge these allegations merely to 'Propaganda.'"

To understand what events and policies eventually led to the Holocaust, atrocities with an unprecedented scale, I was brought back to the year 1933 when Hitler came to power. A campaign against the Jewish people was unleashed– boycott of Jewish business, stripping of all sorts of civil rights by the Nuremberg laws of 1935, and Kristallnacht on November 9, 1938 when more than 1,000 synagogues and over 7,000 Jewish-owned business were vandalized. The exhibit tells us that Gypsies, the handicapped, Poles, homosexuals, Jehovah's witnesses, Soviet prisoners of war and political dissidents were also the victims of Nazi persecution. "Un-German" books were burned and racial purity of "superior" Aryans were to be preserved. Nearly every aspects of German society was subject to Nazification under Hitler's rule.

The entrance to the third floor exhibit was a wooden walkway with a large picture of a ghetto at each side, giving the visitors a feeling that they were about to enter a ghetto and to witness the fate of those who lived there. As the German army advanced into Eastern Europe, Jews were segregated in ghettoes where they had to endure overcrowding, starvation and disease. We can see the actual milk can in which the historians in the Warsaw ghetto hid the documents chronicling ghetto life and buried them deep beneath the street. The can was discovered in1950, realizing the only hope of those who had perished with the ghetto—"the memory of the Warsaw ghetto would endure."[2]

We learn about the tragic yet magnificent end of the Warsaw ghetto—the uprising in the spring of 1943. For more than a month, several hundred Jews armed with meager weapons fought back against thousands of German soldiers until the final liquidation of the ghetto. The last words of Mordecai Anielewicz, the leader of the uprising, read, "The dream of my life has become true. Jewish self defense in the Warsaw ghetto has become a fact. Jewish armed resistance and retaliation have become a reality. I have been a witness to the magnificent heroic struggle of the Jewish fighters." Over 800,000 people died as a result of Ghettoization and general privation.[3]

A rail car…. How many times did I hear about it from many survivors? A hundred people were crammed into this tiny rail car for days without food or water only to be deported to one of the death camps. Inside the rail car, which was donated by the Polish government to the Museum, I could not help but wonder how many victims this tiny rail car alone carried from their home towns to the death camps. Didn't each train go back to yet another small town to pick up victims within a few hours of unloading at a death camp?[4] When I left it, "Selection" was waiting for me. Photographs taken by an SS camp officer show us hundreds of faces of those who had just gotten off the train at Auschwitz. The sick, the elderly, pregnant women, women with young children and children too young to work were to be gassed within hours. But these faces, despite their fear and confusion, did not know what awaited them.

We know exactly what happened to those people by looking at a scale model of the killing process at Auschwitz. Nearly 2,000 victims at a time were processed—undressed, deceived to be showered, gassed, dead within 15 minutes, all gold teeth and fillings removed, shaved off the hair, and finally burned in the crematorium. The model shows individual faces of the victims—"terror-stricken people in their desperate and futile attempt to reach up toward the last air in the gas chamber."[5] Three million victims—men, women, and children—perished in the Nazi camps.[6]

Those who survived the first selection, would go under the gate which said "Arbeit Macht Frei" (work makes you free.) Here, we can listen to the audio testimonies of Auschwitz survivors telling us their experience of terror, brutality, and despair. Whenever I listen to testimonies of Holocaust survivors I am always moved by the dignity and compassion in their voices. Between two barbed wire fence posts from Auschwitz, we can read and almost hear the voice of 15-year-old Elie Wiesel, the most famous Auschwitz survivor, without whose vision as the chairman of the President's Commission on the Holocaust and later the chairman of the United States Holocaust Memorial Council this museum would not have been built:

> Never shall I forget that night, the first night in camp, which has turned my life into one long night, seven times cursed and seven

times sealed. Never shall I forget that smoke. Never shall I forget the little faces of the children, whose bodies I saw turned into wreaths of smoke beneath the blue sky.

Never shall I forget those flames which consumed my faith forever.

Never shall I forget that nocturnal silence which deprived me, for all eternity, of the desire to live. Never shall I forget those moments which murdered my God and my soul and turned my dreams to dust. Never shall I forget these things, even if I am condemned to live as long as God himself. Never.

A U.S. Air Force intelligence photograph of Auschwitz-Birkenau taken in 1944 shows the existence of crematoria there. Yet, we are told that the United States did not try to bomb them although it had a capability of doing so. We are reminded that Americans were bystanders when these terrible crimes were taking place.

One of the most remarkable exhibits in the Museum is the three story tower display of photographs of the residents in a small Jewish town in what is now Lithuania. Unlike other images of Jewish people during the Holocaust, these photographs describe a vibrant Jewish community which existed for 900 years. Every photograph could have been found in our family album—many portraits and photographs taken during everyday life, family gathering and friends get-together. A brief text on the wall tells us that an SS mobile killing squad murdered 4,000 residents from this town and surrounding area in just two days in 1941, and today no Jews live in this town. Nazis killed more than 1,300,000 victims by open-air shootings as did in this town.[7]

On the second floor, visitors can learn about the Righteous Gentiles, non-Jews who risked their lives to rescue Jews. We see famous names like Raoul Wallenberg and Chiune Sugihara and many other not-so-famous names of unsung heroes of the Holocaust. We also learn about Jewish resistance to the Nazi persecution in the ghettoes and in the forests. They would not be led like sheep to the slaughter.[8]

Drawings by children in the Terezin (near Prague) ghetto are the saddest reminder of 1.5 million children who perished in the Holocaust, and of their potential and promise lost in them. President Vaclav Havel described these drawings, "There is only a shadow of grief and anxiety in them, there is much more about dreams of springs, of flowers, butterflies, birds, and also a great longing to be happy and carefree."[9]

Visitors conclude their walk through the permanent exhibit by watching "Testimony"—a film consisting of short interviews with survivors. When I was there, a gentleman on the screen remembered his fellow inmate's prayer. When he heard his friend thanking God, he asked him what he could possibly be thankful for in a concentration camp. His friend answered, "I thanked God for not letting me be a perpetrator of this terrible crime."

After the tour, I sat in the Hall of Remembrance, a large hexagonal room with its Eternal Flame commemorating Jewish and non-Jewish victims of the Holocaust. The hall was full of April daylight coming through its skylight, yet filled with serene silence. Inscribed on the wall were the names of the Nazi concentration and death camps—Auschwitz, Treblinka, Belzec, Sobibor.... Then, I saw a group of young people coming into the Hall. They must have just finished walking through the permanent exhibit. Some of them went to the Eternal Flame and read the biblical quotation on the wall behind it, "...you shall make them known to your children and to your children's children." Watching young people in this sacred Hall of Remembrance was heartwarming. I thought it was a beautiful sight.

As a federal institution, the Museum is governed by the United States Holocaust Memorial Council whose members are appointed by the President of the United States. I interviewed the current Council chairman, Mr. Miles Lerman, after my visit to the Museum.

May I ask about your background?

> I was born in Poland. At the beginning of 1939, I was in the city of Lvov which was occupied by the Soviet Union because of the Ribbentrop-Molotov agreement. Then in June of 1941, Nazi Germany invaded the Soviet Union and I was taken to a slave camp. Our job was to dismantle the gravestones of an old Jewish cemetery and break it up into gravel for building of the roads for advancement of Nazi war machines.

How old were you at that time?

I was twenty-one. It was a very large cemetery, one of the oldest in Poland. It was a pitiful thing to do, you see, you could tell all the history of Jewish people in Lvov from these gorgeous gravestones. When we finished dismantling this cemetery I was transferred to a quarry where we were mining stones. One day, five of us were far away from the main group of people of about 200. We decided to escape. Two Ukrainian policemen were guarding us. We managed to overcome them and got their rifles. We escaped into the forest. And within a period of about three months, we had assembled a group of young men and women consisting of 380 people.

So you did not join a resistance group, but started one.

Yes, we started the group. We lived in the forest and fought the Nazis for 23 months. Of course you understand the objective of the partisan was not to engage in a fight with an army. With meager weapons and ammunitions, you don't take on an army. But we were very effective in raiding their food supplies and petroleum supplies and so on.

You said you fought for 23 months. But what were the odds for partisan fighters to survive in the forest that long in those days?

Well, the odds were very little.

Were they all Jewish people?

We had some Russian prisoners of war joining us, but it was a predominantly Jewish group. We fought side by side with Polish partisan groups. In July of 1944, the Russian army and Polish army advanced and we were liberated. I returned to Lvov on the top of a Russian tank with a machine gun in my hands, and it was a very special and emotional moment.

What did you see there?

When I returned to my home town, this used to be a town where 16,000 Jews had lived, eleven people were found alive.

Only eleven people?

Yes, eleven out of 16,000. The rest of them were murdered, among them were my mother, my sister, her husband and her children and many many members of my family. It was very difficult for me to live there any more because the memories were terribly bitter. So I moved to a city called Lodz, the second largest city in Poland. Even though the war was over, those were dangerous times for the Jews because anti-Semitism was still there. So we decided to immigrate to either Israel or to any of the Western countries. We smuggled across the Polish border into Berlin. Berlin at that time was divided by the four superpowers and we wound up in the American sector. We lived in the displaced person's camp for six months or so.

You started saying "we." Were you married by then?

Yes, I got married after the war. She was a survivor of Auschwitz. I wanted to go to Israel, but my wife told me that she was pregnant. In those days, the British were preventing people from coming to Israel, and those who were intercepted were put in the detention camp in Cyprus. My wife felt that being pregnant and to go behind the wires again, she just came out of Auschwitz, would be too much. So we applied for American visas and came here in 1947.

How did you feel when you landed on the American shore?

The experience in America was fabulous. Having gone through the bitter experience, mass murder, watching the Jewish communities of Europe being wiped off the surface of the earth and a total annihilation, we came to America. People received us well and opportunities were there. We both took jobs and started building our lives all over again.

But what about your past? Did you want to forget it and put it behind you?

No, I did not feel that I could put it behind me. I felt that the impact of this period was of such enormous magnitude that it could not be put behind. I felt that we owed it to those who had perished to make sure that the world remember them. I personally believed that it was necessary that the world understands what human beings are capable of doing under certain circumstances. Of course we came here with nothing. I had to work for my family; by then our daughter was born. But, things gradually started improving and I became very much interested in public life because I felt that by the mere fact that I had survived I owed something to those who didn't.

Was that a general feeling among those who survived and came to America?

I must tell you that most people were reluctant to talk about it. There were even survivors who had psychological difficulties dealing with that period. They were hoping that they would be able to brush it under the carpet and it would go away. But these memories were so bitter, so shocking and so devastating that they didn't go away. They were suppressed. It was a way of psychological denial. But I and my wife, I must give her a lot of credit, strongly felt that we owed it to those who perished that they should be remembered. As we started to speak about it, more and more survivors began to come out and talked about it.

And you were involved in building the Holocaust Museum from the very beginning?

Yes. President Carter appointed Mr. Elie Wiesel as chairman of the President's Commission on the Holocaust in 1978. After a short deliberation we came back to the President and told him that if there was anything we did not want, it would be a monument. We wanted a museum that would be a living and teaching museum, a museum that would teach and sensitize visitors as to what could happen to mankind if they let their guard down.

I have just visited the Museum and was very impressed. It was indeed a profound experience. But did you envision from the very beginning that you would be able to create this kind of museum?

No. I must tell you that the period of searching for the most suitable way to create the museum was more taxing than building it. I remember nights and days of hard discussions, debates and arguments. There were those who argued that Americans would not be able to face it. Or others would argue that Americans would not be interested in coming to such a museum. And the other debates were how we would do it. Do we tell the whole story? Do we just insinuate? Do we go gently about it? Do we just lay out the facts? There were ongoing debates and those who insisted that the history should be told as it actually happened prevailed.

Throughout those debates what was the uniting force that would ultimately lead to that final decision?

I would say that the more we talked about it, the more we discussed it, and the more we were together, the more we became convinced that this was the chapter in history that could not be forgotten. This must be recorded not only for the past but also for the future. The museum must serve as a warning and as a means of sensitizing the people that the civility of human beings is skin deep. You scratch a little bit of your skin and a pretty ugly creature comes out.

That is a very scary thought.

Yes, a pretty ugly creature. So, we quickly realized that unless we would have irrefutable evidence, unless we would have archives and artifacts by which to convince the visiting public that this was what actually happened, nobody would believe us. We needed to go out and to accumulate as many archives as we could. I was appointed at that time as chairman of the Committee of International Relations. These were the days when the Eastern European nations were still Communist. We started negotiating for a formal agreement first with the government of Poland and later the Soviet Union, Hungary, Czechoslovakia and so on.

Were they difficult negotiations?

Very difficult. Because they were Communist regimes. When you talk about getting access to their archives, I don't have to tell you how they reacted. So it was a difficult thing to convince them that we were not after politics but we were after history. And it is the history that should be of interest to them just as much as to us because Poles also suffered from the Nazi occupation. Finally we succeeded. They realized that my intentions were genuine and not political. They realized that it would be good for them, too. There were some decent people in Poland who recognized that as a country where 95% of its Jewish population was wiped out they had a moral obligation to remember them.

So the collecting archival materials was basically done by convincing them, not by any sort of political negotiation?

Yes. No political pressure. Just by telling them how important it was—this is a chapter of the history of mankind that must serve as a lesson for future generations.

I read that the signing ceremony between the U.S. and Poland took place in your native town which became the site of a death camp. Can you tell me about it?

Yes. The Polish government gave me a choice of where to sign the agreement. Instead of Warsaw, the capital, I would much rather sign this agreement on the site of the death camp called Belzec, where my family were murdered. I remember more than three thousand people gathered at the ceremony. I am not a historian but just a business man. So once the agreement was signed, our archivists and historians could start researching on the Nazi crimes in Poland. Then I decided to negotiate with the Soviet Union.

This was still before the collapse of the Soviet Union?

Yes. I thought that if I break through with the Soviet Union other communist countries would follow. So I started working in Washington through the Russian Embassy. Mr. Dobrynin was the ambassador to the United States at that time. He was a very smart man and spoke fluent English. I remember my first meeting with him very well. He asked me all kinds of questions— what my objective was , what I was interested in learning, where I would like to go in the Soviet Union and so on. I gave him answers and he told me to come back in three weeks. After three weeks I came back and sat down with him—same thing. He asked me the same questions and I gave the same answers. He said, "I will get in touch with Moscow, come back in a month." After one month he and I sat down again and the same thing happened. I became puzzled, so I finally asked, "Mr. Ambassador this is my third visit to you and you are asking me the same questions. May I submit to you that my interest is history and not politics. What I am interested in, you should be interested in, too, because the Soviet Union suffered tremendously from the Nazi Germany." He looked at me and said, "Mr. Lerman, everything is politics."

You said that you were just a businessman. But it seems that you were doing more than a diplomat could do.

Well, I was determined that we needed to accumulate archives. We needed to have documents. Telling the history without substantiating it is not going to do. We needed to have access to their national archives where they had the documents captured when they had driven the Nazis out. The communications between Berlin and Kiev ordering round up of the Jews and liquidating them. The documents of the looting of the valuables, gold and silver. The reports to Berlin of how many Jews were killed at such and such places on such and such dates, among them how many men, women and children. They were crazy that they recorded their crimes in every detail. Perhaps they were convinced that they would win the war and those would be the pages of their glorious history.

So, after Ambassador Dobrynin told me that everything was politics, I still maintained that what we were interested in was history, the history that should interest his country also. He told me to come back in one week.

This time it was one week. Then what happened?

He set up an appointment for me with the office of the main archives of the Soviet Union, which was a part of the Politburo. I took a group of historians and archivists with me to Moscow and spent several days negotiating. We finally succeeded in getting an agreement. They gave us four cities to work in, Moscow, Riga, Vilna and Lvov. Since their archives operate under a different system than ours it has been a very slow process, we are still working. As a matter of fact, just six months ago the present Russian government transferred to us 15,000 KGB documents. This is of enormous importance because these documents substantiate the crimes with a greater dimension. After the Soviet Union, negotiations went a lot easier with other countries—Czechoslovakia, Hungary and East Germany. As a result of these negotiations, I would venture to say that we are today one of the largest repositories of archival data dealing with the Reich, the fall of Nazi Germany, and all aspects of the annihilation of the Jews and other victims of the Holocaust.

I heard that you were also in charge of raising the necessary funds to build the Museum.

Yes. The land for the Museum was a gift from the United States government. And both houses of Congress voted us into a law as a federal institution. It was with a clear understanding that all the necessary funds, for the building and the equipping of the Museum, must come from the private sectors of America. So we started campaigning. Again, the same story. There were many doubts and many people were saying to us, "You are dreaming. You will not be able to get funds from the people. They will not be interested in this." I had a personal friend with whom I had worked at another organization who told me, "Miles, you are heading for a failure. You will need an enormous amount of money, 200 million dollars, and you'll just not be able to get it."

You assumed the responsibility of raising funds voluntarily. Why?

Because I felt very strongly that the Museum must be built. It took us six years. But funds came from all walks of life, from Jews and non-Jews, from rich and poor, we even had children who brought their piggy banks. It cost us more to process their donation than actual amount they brought in. But these were the most precious gifts and I always choked up when children came with their piggy banks.

And the Museum finally opened in 1993.

Yes. And again, there were many doubts if the American people would be interested in this subject matter until the very last minutes. But when we opened up, it was like a floodgate opening up. We estimated that under the best circumstances we would get between 4 and 5 hundred thousand visitors a year. In reality we got 2 million a year. This is very heartwarming because it was a vision, it was a dream that became a reality. This is not one person's effort. Many many good people took part in building of the Museum. I am very proud and very fulfilled. What we are doing is sensitizing the visitors about this terrible period of history, about the importance of looking out and always being on guard against hatred of any kind. We are a wonderful country but hatred did not disappear from anywhere in the world, neither did it here. Look at the Oklahoma bombing, it's frightening. When we opened the Museum we made it our business not only to deal with the past and to remember the victims of the Nazis, but to be on the forefront of any act of genocide. So when the civil war broke out in former Yugoslavia we were the first ones to raise an alarm about it.

So the Committee on Conscience was finally set up.

Yes, we organized it and it's functioning now. We have the Committee on Conscience which consists of leading members of the Council and the nation's moral leaders. We are very much conscious of the genocidal threats that are taking place today, and we'll do everything possible to prevent it.

So all the dreams you had came true.

Well, I am very proud of what we have achieved. I feel very rewarded with the accomplishments. I believe that this alone was worth my having survived. The reality has proven that the visitors to the Museum are very much interested in what they see, they want to come back, and they want to learn more. This year alone we are working with 36,000 teachers that bring groups of high school students to the Museum. All in all, I can tell you that we have created a temple of memory that we are very proud of.

We have very excellent staff who are dedicated and the Museum is growing. I am very pleased that fate has put me in its path and that I should play a role in this.

For many Japanese, the Holocaust is so distant an event in terms of where it happened and to whom it happened, that they have a hard time understanding that this actually happened to our fellow human beings. Aside from visiting this Museum, do you have any suggestion for Japanese people as to how they can learn the lessons from the history of the Holocaust?

Let me answer you this way. I would like an opportunity to go and lecture in Japan. If I was invited by a large organization or a university I would accept the invitation. Very much so. Your country had a militaristic and expansionistic past and you saw to what it led. I always maintain that perpetrators do not only consume their victims. Soon or later they consume themselves. Your country also had a terrible experience with the atomic-bombs which was a traumatic experience. I am not so sure that America will go down in history being very proud of this. I love America and admire this country. I want you to know that. But I am not so sure about this chapter as a proud moment in the history of America. But most importantly, what your country has shown is by shaking off its militarism and shaking off its very dogmatic idea of being a super being that has a right to dominate the Far East, you had chosen a path of peace. And take a look at how far you have gotten! A tremendous growth economically and intellectually. This is why I am so puzzled. How can a country like this gobble up such garbage of anti-Semitic books?

I think a part of it is ignorance.

I am talking about the intellectual community.

I think Japanese intellectuals all know that those books are garbage. The problem is that they don't speak out.

Well, that is the one of the lessons that you learn in this museum. If there is anything that we have learned from those terrible years, that is for good and decent people to stand by and not to speak out is tantamount to being a part of the crime. If I was invited to speak in Japan I would address the issue straightforward.

A few months before I interviewed Mr. Lerman, I had seen him on TV. It was the night before the Presidential inauguration, and the Holocaust Museum was hosting an event celebrating American democracy. I heard him saying that he never would have dreamt of addressing such an occasion when he was fighting in the forest as a Jewish partisan.

I remember reading somewhere that for the Jews "resistance was never, and could not have been, a strategy for survival. It was an existential act of honor and courage in the face of certain death."[10] When I interviewed Mr. Lerman he did not talk much about those days. But I saw that honor and courage still very much alive in him after 52 years.

NOTES

[1] Jeshajahu Weinberg and Rina Ellieli, *The Holocaust Museum in Washington* (New York: Rizzoli International Publications, Inc., 1995), 23.

[2] Michael Berenbaum, *The World Must Know* (New York: Little Brown and Company, 1993), 92.

[3] Raul Hilberg, *The Destruction of the European Jews* (New York: Holmes & Meier Publishers, Inc., 1985), 338.

[4] Caude Lanzmann, *Shoah* (New York: Da Capo Press, 1995), 130.

[5] Edward T. Linenthal, *Preserving Memory: The Struggle to Create America's Holocaust Museum* (New York: Viking Penguin, 1995), 210.

[6] Hilberg, *The Destruction of the European Jews*, 338.

[7] Hilberg, *The Destruction of the European Jews*, 338.

[8] Berenbaum, *The World Must Know,* 174.

[9] Hana Volavkova, ed. *I Never Saw Another Butterfly.* United States Holocaust Memorial Museum, 2nd ed. (New York: Schocken Books, 1993), 104.

[10] Berenbaum, *The World Must Know*, 177.

I Can't Understand the Event,
Therefore, I Will Try

Dr. Michael Berenbaum
President and CEO
The Survivors of the Shoah Visual History Foundation

Dr. Michael Berenbaum was the project director of the United States Holocaust Memorial Museum and later served as the director of the Research Institute of the same institution. Currently, he is the President and Chief Executive Officer of Survivors of the Shoah Visual History Foundation created by Steven Spielberg in 1994.

He was born in the United States in 1945, some three months after the liberation of the Nazi camps, yet his life has been profoundly affected by the Holocaust. At age of sixteen, he visited Israel's Yad Vashem, the Jewish national memorial to the *Shoah*, and "was moved to tears and touched in the indelible way that high school students can be touched by tragedy."[1] In 1967, when the Six Day War was about to begin, he left for Israel "to be with his people." He did not want to be on the sidelines, a bystander—whether passive or active—as Jewish history was being lived.[2] After coming back to the United States, he wrote his doctoral dissertation on Elie Wiesel and later worked for him when President Carter appointed Mr. Wiesel to chair the President's Commission on the Holocaust in 1978.

Dr. Berenbaum was responsible first for articulating the task of the Commission and the Holocaust Memorial Council, its successor body, and then for actually carrying out that task—creating the United States Holocaust Memorial Museum in Washington, D.C. He wrote in 1981:

In my opinion, the task of the Holocaust Memorial Council involves the Americanization of the Holocaust; that is, the story
must be told in such a way that it resonates not only with the
survivor in New York, his son in Houston or his daughter in San
Francisco, but with the Black leader from Atlanta and his child,
the farmer from the Midwest, the Industrialist from the North-
east, and the millions of other Americans who each year make a
pilgrimage to Washington to visit their nation's capital. The Americanization of the Holocaust is an honorable task provided that
the story told is truthful, faithfully representing the historical
event in a way that can be grasped by an American audience.[3]

He wrote the story line for the permanent exhibit of the Holocaust
Museum, which was also made into a one volume book "The World
Must Know" whose Japanese translation became available in 1996.

I visited him at the Shoah Foundation where he recently took up
his new challenge of creating a digital database of recorded testimonies of the Holocaust survivors.

*I know we will never be able to find a satisfactory answer to this ques-
tion, but for the Japanese readers who typically do not have deep a knowledge about the Holocaust, can you explain the commonly accepted views
as to why this tragedy happened?*

That's a profound question, not a simple question. Let me give
you a variety of different views as to why it happened. I'll begin
with theology. Hitler tried to establish himself as a God. He
thought of establishing a thousand year Reich, and a part of what
happened was he had to slaughter the other Gods. The easiest
way to destroy Christianity was to destroy the mother religion
Judaism not the daughter religion. And therefore to eliminate
Judaism he tried to eliminate Jews, that was a part of his idolatry.

There's another way of saying it, which is that one of the greatest
issues in the world today is how we deal with the "superfluous
population," those who have no rightful place in society. Now, I
don't think of "rights" in American term, but I think of "rights"
in terms of an ability to fend for themselves. What Germans did
was to essentially define one population as superfluous and then
take the most radical solution for the "superfluous population,"

which is their wholesale elimination, their extermination and their murder.

It began ironically with the mentally retarded, physically disabled and emotionally disturbed. And the "Final Solution to the Jewish problem" was designed to eliminate all Jews from the face of the earth. The Jew was the outsider in the European culture. The Jew was what you call in sociological terms "cognitively dissident," who did not fit in to the rest of the society and represented itself as being negated from the rest of the society. A part of what the Nazis did was to eliminate them by a wholesale slaughter.

There was a continuity between the elimination of the Jews and the totality of Western European history. Christians said, "You have no right to live among us as Jews, therefore convert." Rulers in Spain in 1492 said, "You have no right to live among us, therefore leave." And Hitler said, "You have no right to live, therefore die."[4] Essentially what was involved here was precisely population elimination which was continuity in direction from the rest of European civilization.

I also think that it had something to do with the proving of the master race. What Hitler did was to have a racist ideology which saw a master race, a series of subservient races, and one race that was unworthy of living, Jews.

Those are a few of the answers as to why the Holocaust happened.

You have written about the uniqueness and universality of the Holocaust. What is unique and what is universal about the Holocaust?

The Holocaust differs from all previous manifestations of anti-Semitism. First, most previous manifestations of anti-Semitism were episodic. They came for a time and passed. The Holocaust was a sustained government policy for 12 years.

Secondly, most anti-Semitism took place outside of the law, they were out-law phenomena. The Holocaust used the instrumentality of the law as the means of destruction. The Nazis took the law and used it as a way in which they destroyed Jews.

Thirdly, most manifestations of anti-Semitism were geographically local. If you were in trouble in Spain you had freedom in Portugal, and if you were in trouble in Portugal you could find heaven in Holland. The Holocaust took place on the entire continent of Europe.

Finally, in all previous manifestations of anti-Semitism, Jews were killed for what they were, for identity they formed, for values they practiced and religious beliefs they held. Under Nazism Jews were killed not because of what they were but because of the fact that they were. They killed Jews on the basis of blood.

What makes the Holocaust unique in world history is that it is the first time in world history that you had the elimination of an entire population—men, women and children—regarded as the national goal and essential to the national salvation of another people. This was not a limited genocide, it was a total genocide. The word was "the final solution" of the Jewish problem, "final" meaning once and for all and "solution" means that problems would never again occur.

So, that's unique. Plus even the instrumentality by which the Nazi killed the Jews was unique. You have a movement in evolution of killing from, for example, definition to mobile killing units. Mobile killing units entailed sending killers to the victims. What made the Holocaust unique is what then happened. After the Nazis sent the killers to the victims, they found that was difficult for the killers. They had too much human contact with the victims. So what they then did was to just reverse it. That is you had stationary killing centers and mobile victims. The essential instrumentality was the railroad car which took the Jews from the ghettoes to the death camps. Essentially what you had was the factory, mass-industrialized death factory whose end product was killing.

Take for example the death camp of Belzec. Belzec was open for a period of ten months, and 600,000 people were killed there during that ten months by a staff of 14 Germans and 102 Ukrainians. The total number of Jews killed was 600,000 with only five known survivors, of whom two had ever testified on what they had witnessed. So, you had a mass industrialized killing center, which was unique, with the gas chamber and the crematoria.

And the final point. Human history had known slavery, but what the Nazis did was to take human slavery to a new level. In American slavery, which was awful, a slave was considered a capital investment. To give you a simple example of capital investment, if you have a car what do you do with your car. All of us put gasoline in the car. Most of us who are smart enough change the oil. Almost all of us occasionally wash the car. That's what you do with capital investment. You protect it and you preserve it. Nazism was unique in that slavery was considered not capital investment but consumable raw material to be discarded in the process, manufactured and recycled. So slaves were not fed, they weren't offered shelter, they weren't offered clothing, and they weren't offered living conditions. When they died, their body parts were recycled. That never happened in human history.

And why was it universal? Its universality was precisely because it was not done by the least cultured of Western societies, but it was done by the most cultured and "most civilized" of Western societies. Therefore, it implicates all of Western civilization.

Can you elaborate on that?

All it means is that there are elements in Western civilization that can use the brilliance of technological innovations for destructive purposes. It means that there's not enough restraint that protects us from dehumanization.

I visited the Holocaust Memorial Museum in Washington, D.C. and was profoundly impressed. I know you were responsible for creating the story line for the exhibit. What was the most difficult part of that assignment?

The most difficult part was to find a way of speaking directly, truthfully, profoundly and openly about the evil involved without becoming a chamber of horrors. The most difficult part was to find a way of personalizing stories so it was not abstract but it was concrete. That was what we thought would be the most difficult part, but it was answered by the survivors. They became the instrument by which we told the story. Survivors enabled us to comprehend the terrible story of the Holocaust through the very particular lens of the individuals who lived it.

You wrote that what you were trying to do was an Americanization of the Holocaust. Do you think the success of the Museum was due to the fact that this nation was built on what American people consider to be universal ideals?

I had to translate the Holocaust into the American idiom. I was asked to create the Holocaust Museum in Washington, D.C. in the middle of the shrines of the United States of America. I had to relate to American society.

So, there can be "Japanization" of the Holocaust?

It is inevitable that when a country grappled with the experience it sees it through the lens of their civilization. I think it is a perfectly normal function of cultural absorption. People with different history and different backgrounds approach the Holocaust differently. For example, the German approach to the Holocaust is different than that of Jews. The Christian approach is different from the Moslem's because it's more linked to Christianity than it is to Islam. A person in Western civilization approaches it differently than someone who is not part of Western civilization.

Japan should approach it differently from other societies because the issues are different. The Holocaust says something a little bit less to Japanese society than it does to us, but may say something to Japan as it becomes more and more westernized.

And of course we have a tradition of strong bureaucracy and a tendency to act as a group rather than as individuals, both of which, I think, have commonality with some of the elements in the Holocaust.

Yes. And there is a sense of xenophobia. Japan is a much more uniform society than, for example, the United States. One of the issues raised by the Holocaust is what is the limit of universal responsibility. Whom am I responsible for? Am I responsible only for myself? Only for my family? Only for my tribe? Only for those who are part of my religion? Or is the universal responsibility much larger? The difference between the rescuers and the perpetrators was that the rescuers regarded the Jews as human beings just like they were.

In trying to understand and draw universal lessons from the Holocaust, how can we overcome the notion of "those of us who were not there will never understand."?

The survivors who lived this event have seen the dimension of humanity, of government, of culture and civilization, and even of divinity of "God" that is radically different than what you and I understand and experienced in all of our lives. Their eyes have seen something very distinct and unprecedented.

We may understand 90 percent of it and part of it eludes us. But eluding us should only happen at the end, not at the beginning. You can't begin by saying, "I can't understand the event." You have to begin by saying, "I can't understand the event, therefore, I will try."

Can I ask about Survivors of the Shoah Visual History Foundation? What are the goals and how do you try to achieve them?

There's a short term goal and a long term goal. The short term goal is to take 50,000 testimonies. Fifty thousand is not a magic number but it means a substantive number of testimonies of living witnesses to the event, namely survivors. We want to take them, then digitize them, and make them available to at least five repositories. (Four in the U.S. and in Jerusalem) Once we make them available we then will want people to look at this material in educational ways and other ways toward developing curricula to teach tolerance.

Essentially what we are doing is a people's history of the event. History is usually written by the people who had played a historical role or who were the elite who wrote memoirs and documents. This is a people's history of the event designed to tell the story through the eyes of those who saw it. That's a short term goal.

Our long term goal is to use this instrumentality for teaching and to create a language for teaching history in the 21st century. They will learn outside the classroom in multiple ways with the films, maps, music and documentary materials. This in an attempt to use this as linchpins for different types of education.

How many languages are used in interviews?

We are working in 29 languages in 44 countries.

I heard some survivors are interviewers also.

Survivors have been enormously helpful to us, they've been enormously gracious to us. They trusted us. They work as volunteers at the Foundation, some even serve as interviewers. We could not be where we are without the trust of survivors.

Will these materials be available in Japanese so that Japanese students can also use this technology?

We did a couple of interviews in Japan related to the Sugihara story. So we are hoping that this material will be available for Japanese students either in translational captions or directly in Japanese.

I think it is wonderful that one private citizen such as Mr. Spielberg, with his talent and resources, can start this kind of project and contribute to the society and future generations. I would like to see this type of philanthropic spirit take root in Japan.

I hope so, too.

Dr. Berenbaum wrote both in the introduction and in the conclusion for *The World Must Know*, "I have told you this story not to weaken you. But to strengthen you. Now it is up to you!"[5] While working on this project I returned to this book countless times. Having been deeply impressed by the exhibit at the Holocaust Memorial Museum which he had created, I somehow assumed that he was a person who became very strong through his work on the Holocaust. When I finally met him, however, I didn't find a person I had expected. Rather, I found a person who, it seemed to me, was still struggling. Dr. Berenbaum told me, "Dealing with the Holocaust is not easy."

While driving back home I kept saying those words to myself— "Dealing with the Holocaust is not easy..." And I knew that the next question he would have asked me was whether I could say, "Therefore, I will try to understand."

NOTES

[1]Michael Berenbaum, "Transforming the Void," in *From the Unthinkable to the Unavoidable*, ed. Carol Rittner and John K. Roth (Westport, CT: Praeger, 1997), 174.

[2]Ibid., 176.

[3]Michael Berenbaum, "The Uniqueness and Universality of the Holocaust," in *Holocaust: Religious and Philosophical Implications*, ed. John K. Roth and Michael Berenbaum (New York: Paragon House, 1989), 85.

[4]Raoul Hilberg, *The Destruction of the European Jews* (Chicago: Quadrangle Books Inc., 1961), 3-4.

[5]Michael Berenbaum, *The World Must Know* (Boston: Little Brown and Company, 1993), 3, 223.

Restoring Justice and Building Bridges
Between Peoples

Simon Wiesenthal
Holocaust survivor, Nazi-hunter

I never expected the Mauthausen concentration camp to be located on such a beautiful hill. Below it was a sleepy little village with a white church. It was in 1938, right after the German annexation of Austria, that the Nazis started building a concentration camp at Mauthausen located about 30 miles east of Linz, a city in Upper Austria where Adolf Hitler spent his childhood years. Initially, it was for political prisoners. Then in 1942, as more and more Jews from the occupied areas in Eastern Europe and prisoners of war arrived, a gas chamber and crematorium were installed. The gassing continued until only a week before it was liberated by the American Forces in May of 1945. It was recorded that almost 30,000 inmates had died between January and May of that year.[1] Peter van Pels, whose adolescent romance with Anne Frank was chronicled by her, also died here only a few days before the liberation.[2]

On one afternoon in November, 1996, I visited Mauthausen, "the death hill,"[3] to see the place where Simon Wiesenthal, the famed Nazi hunter, had started his journey for justice. Although I had just met a very energetic Wiesenthal on the previous day, the image that kept coming back as I walked the memorial site of Mauthausen was that of a person who weighed only 90 pounds and could barely walk. He himself described the day when he was liberated 51 years ago.

"It was ten o'clock on the morning of May 5 1945 when I saw a big, gray tank with a white star on its side and the American flag waving from the turret. I stood on the windswept square that had been, until an hour earlier, the courtyard of the Mauthausen concentration camp. The day was sunny, with a scent of spring in the air. Gone was the sweetish smell of burnt flesh that had always hovered over the yard....The tank with the white star was about a hundred yards in front of me. I wanted to touch the star, but I was too weak. I had survived to see this day, but I couldn't make the last hundred yards...."[4]

What the American soldiers saw at Mauthausen on that day was indeed "the death hill." They found nearly ten thousand bodies in a huge communal grave. Of the 110,000 survivors, thousands were dying before the eyes of the Americans.[5] Fred Friendly, a young war correspondent, wrote his mother from Mauthausen.

"I saw the shower room where 150 prisoners at a time were disrobed and ordered in for a shower which never gushed forth from the sprinklers because the chemical was gas. When they ran out of gas, they merely sucked all of the air out of the room. I talked to the Jews who worked in the crematory, one room adjacent, where six and seven bodies at a time were burned. They gave these jobs to Jews because they all died anyhow. I saw emaciated bodies in piles like cords of wood. I saw the living skeletons, some of whom, regardless of our medical corp's work, will die. I saw the look in their eyes."[6]

When I visited Mauthausen, the gas chamber and the crematorium Friendly had seen were still there as well as the chimney through which the smoke of death had filled the air. I went to the commandant room into which Wiesenthal had dragged himself just a few days after the liberation. Later, he described what took place in this room.

Having struggled for breath for a minute, I was able to speak: 'I was beaten.' 'By whom?' 'By a block clerk.' 'A SS man?' 'No, a prisoner.' The American officer before me regarded me uncomprehendingly: this man went through hell, he can scarcely stand up he's so weak, and he struggles up this hill to complain about a few blows. Blows not even from a Nazi. He didn't understand: it was just because the Third Reich had collapsed three days before that these blows hurt. Because I was determined never again—never again—to let myself be beaten by another person....Colonel Seibel had ordered the Polish block clerk to be brought before him and this had given me the assurance that right and justice were once more supreme on earth. Without being aware of it, he contributed significantly to my recapturing the meaning of my life: to help restore justice by bringing to trial those who had humiliated, tortured and murdered my companions in the ghettos and my fellow prisoners in the concentration camps."[7]

Across the commandant room was a vast courtyard (garage yard), where thousands of newly arrived inmates were striped naked, even in winter[8], and told that they were not human beings any more. "Dehumanization was an important part of the administration of the concentration camps," Professor Willnauer, my guide on that day who was teaching the history of the Holocaust at Teacher's College in Linz, told me.

It was that human dignity, however, that Wiesenthal, after having been transported among 13 camps and having been so close to death many times, had still retained when he was liberated. And it was precisely this human dignity and justice that he was determined to bring back to those who did not survive. But, how...?

I first learned about Simon Wiesenthal when I visited the Museum of Tolerance in Los Angeles. This hi-tech and hands-on museum run by the Simon Wiesenthal Center tries to teach visitors the history of the Holocaust and the importance of tolerance. More than a million people, including many junior high and high school students, have visited here since it opened its doors in 1993. Many dignitaries—heads of the states, politicians, and human rights activists around the world—also visit this museum. On the second floor, there is an exhibition corner for Simon Wiesenthal with a large picture of him at the center. In addition to a brief description of his life is the goal Wiesenthal has tried to achieve.

> Simon Wiesenthal's work has been driven by one goal—that the world will never forget the men, women and children who lost their lives to the darkest of all evils. For if we remember their souls, bring their murderers to justice, and learn to speak out in the face of discrimination and oppression—we will be providing

a memorial to the victims, a warning to the potential murderers of tomorrow, and a lesson for all humanity.[9]

One can learn there that he was responsible for the arrests of 1,100 former Nazis, including Adolf Eichmann, Franz Stangl, the commandant of the Sobibor and the Treblinka death camps where 900,000 Jews were killed, and the Gestapo officer who arrested the family of Anne Frank. Upon learning these fascinating stories, one can easily create a legendary image out of this relentless Nazi hunter. That was what happened to me when I first saw the exhibit. I asked myself, "What an extraordinary person! But is he real? How could he keep facing the tragedy of the past when everybody else wanted to forget it?" I wanted to meet him in person to find out if he was a real human being just like the rest of us.

So, I visited him at his Documentation Center in Vienna. In his youthful voice, 87-year-old Wiesenthal said, "Welcome," as he extended his hand to me. I felt the warmth of his hand and suddenly found myself standing next to a forceful yet very courteous European gentleman. After letting me sit down on one of the chairs in the room, he sat close to me instead of going back to the chair behind his large desk. Simon Wiesenthal, the legendary Nazi hunter, was sitting only a foot away from me! Before I managed to ask any meaningful questions, he started talking:

> The Holocaust did not come over night. Nazis did not start it with the gas chambers and the crematoria. The hate was hundreds of years old. Nazis gradually took away the rights of Jewish people while spreading the idea that the Jews were sub-human. At the beginning we did not believe that the cultured German people would take a man like Hitler seriously. But when we realized the danger it was already too late. So, it is very important, especially for young people, to understand that hate and intolerance even in seemingly small things can lead to horrible tragedies.
>
> Helping people not to forget can be done not only through books and lectures. I decided to help to bring justice by opening a trial because I believed that that was the only way to make an influence on the murderers of tomorrow. There may have been other possibilities of taking justice into our own hands. But I did not choose them because I knew that revenge does not bring justice.

People often ask me, "How is it possible that you speak so calmly about this terrible matter when you yourself went through it?" I answer to them, "That's because I am not a hater. I cannot hate. You may be able to do what I have been doing only once or twice with hate. Tens of thousands of people are waiting that I accuse an innocent so they can discredit my work. Before I give a document to proper authority or prepare against somebody, I checked, double checked and re-checked. I have lists of 6,000 cases in this documentation center. But, in reality, I have decided to be involved in 1,100 cases. I was not hundred percent sure about the other cases. If I had hated these people my decision would have been different. Of the 1,100 cases I have involved, only four sued me for libel, three lost their cases, and one dropped the charge. So you see you can't do my job with hate.

At this point, I asked the question that had been intriguing me most, "Why have you continued to do your job for 51 years when most people prefer to forget the past?" Wiesenthal then showed me his wrist with a scar. That was the scar from his attempted suicide. He had tried to kill himself when he was faced with an imminent torture by a Nazi officer to make him confess the whereabouts of his partisan friends.

You see, I tried to commit suicide and was very close to death many times. When I was liberated I did not have any family members, one relative or one friend with or for whom I could live. I thought my wife was also dead. So, there were no home or life that I could go back to. I asked the US War Crimes Commission to let me work for them. I needed a few years to find out, though, that the name was a mistake because the crimes of the Nazi had nothing to do with the war. War crimes were committed by all parties during the war. Bombings of the cities and its civilian population were war crimes. But the Nazi Crime was different.

Later, I found out that my wife was also alive, but we lost eighty-nine members of both of our families. I could not go back to a normal life. My wife used to tell me, "You were an architect before the war and you can go back to your profession." The last conversation we had was twelve years ago. She said, "Isn't it enough what you have done? We can go to Israel where our daughter and our grandchildren live." I said to her, "Maybe you are right. We can do that. But, then I would feel like a traitor. Can you live with a traitor?" And that was our last talk about my work'

How does Wiesenthal feel about those former Nazis, who were brought to the court of justice after so many years of leading a normal life? His answer was unequivocal.

> A murderer remains a murderer even if he is hundred years old. But, when you try to bring someone that old to a trial, whole sympathy goes for him. For example, when an 80-year-old former Nazi was tried in Stuttgart a few years ago, there was a demonstration against me. They were saying, "Let this old man die in peace." I told them that he had lost his right to die in peace. I believe it is even more important for the world to know what he had done even if the event took place more than 50 years ago. During the trial, newspapers reported all the details of what this man had done and the world paid attention to the trial. This is what we have to do for our children and their children. I believe that if history can repeat itself, it would be our failures, not those of the future generations. Do you understand?

As he became more passionate, he often repeated the question, "Do you understand?" How many times did he have to repeat this question in the last 51 years? And one nation which ignored and sometimes even attacked him for what he was doing was his own, Austria. Wiesenthal was born in 1908 in Galicia, then the eastern part of the Austro-Hungarian Empire, and later studied architecture in Prague. After surviving the Holocaust, he decided to live in Austria which had proportionately provided more participants to aid in the Nazi's mass murders than did Germany. Wiesenthal chose to live among the murderers. Post-war Austria quickly created for herself a convenient image of being the first victim of the Nazi aggression. Wiesenthal was an unwelcome reminder of her ugly past. In spite of his many achievements abroad, including the US Congressional gold medal which he received from President Carter in 1980, he had to wage a lonely fight in his own country for a long time. Bruno Kreisky, who was a chancellor of Austria from 1970 to 1983, accused Wiesenthal of having collaborated with the Gestapo during the war.[10] Wiesenthal withstood the allegations, but those were the hardest years for him since his survival of the Holocaust. He routinely received threats. After all, there are only 7,000 Jews presently living in Austria, where the overwhelming majority of the population of 8 million is Catholic and where anti-Semitic sentiment is still strong. How would the Japanese society react if there was a world-famous Korean or Chinese person living in Japan who kept tracking down former members of the Japanese Imperial Army that had engaged in crimes?

In recent years, however, Wiesenthal's long fight for justice was finally winning the hearts of his countrymen. In 1994, Chancellor Vranitzky declared that Austria must share responsibility for the Holocaust. He told the world that Austria could no longer hide behind the claim that it had itself been a victim nation. He wrote Wiesenthal that many discussions he had had with him had contributed to his declaration on Austria's Nazi links.[11] Then in 1995, the city of Vienna, where anti-Semitism is hundreds of years old and where young Hitler first discovered the taste of it, gave Wiesenthal an honorary citizenship, a high honor awarded only to a handful of people.[12]

Wiesenthal also maintains a very strong stand on the issue of "hate speech." He told me with this reflection,

> It was a several years ago that I talked to this Jewish American lawyer in Chicago who was defending a neo-Nazi group's right to march in the city on the grounds of the First Amendment. I asked him if he knew that he was an indirect survivor of the Holocaust. I said to him, "If Germany had won the war, their first request to the U.S. would have been the transfer of all the Jews in America. I am a direct survivor of the Holocaust, and you would have been the next." I hope he understood. I remember very well how the Nazi started to use their propaganda against Jews in the 1930s and what it led to. I don't want to see that happen again. I have been telling senators and congressmen that we need a law against racist propaganda. We still can have freedom of speech.'

Wiesenthal's determination to condemn those who deny the Holocaust is even stronger. He never will forget the remark made by an SS man during the war, "You would tell the Americans about the German

concentration camps after the war, but they would not believe you."[13]
Today he is determined to tell the history of the Holocaust and the
lesson it has taught, especially to young people. He explained,

> Well, today I can't ignore my age. So I only accept the invita-
> tions to speak to young people. High school students are also
> visiting this office every week. I teach them about the idea of
> justice and friendship. You see, friendship is a holy matter. I have
> looked for the perpetrators of all the victims, not just Jews. Not
> all the Jews understood this. The next victims may not be Jews.
> And what did we see in Yugoslavia and in Africa? The victims
> were not Jews.

True to his words that he would never retire, Wiesenthal continues
to speak out against hatred and intolerance. When the Freedom Party,
Austria's right-wing party whose leader was considered by many Aus-
trians a demagogic populist, gained considerable popularity recently,
Wiesenthal warned of the danger of populism reminding people how
the world failed to recognize the danger of the Nazi party in the early
1930s.[14]

My conversation with Wiesenthal ended with his long-held belief. "Crimes should be tried against the individual not against a whole
country or a group of people. I personally knew that there were some
Nazis who were decent human beings."

"Shall we go now?" Professor Willnauer asked me as I looked at
the beautiful sun setting behind the picturesque village down the
hill. I was thinking about the inmates who must have seen the same
sunset. He suggested that we go to the village, adding that he grew
up there during the war. And in no time, we arrived at the white
church that we had spotted from Mauthausen. In the front yard,
there was a war memorial, on which a few dozen names were inscribed. It was surrounded by beautiful flowers. "They were from
this village, those who fought and died in both WWI and WWII,"
Professor Willnauer explained to me. I couldn't help but think about
the very poignant sentences from *Sunflower*, Wiesenthal's war time
memoir, where he described his feeling upon passing by a military
cemetery as he walked to a labor camp.

Suddenly I envied the dead soldiers. Each had a sunflower to connect him with the living world, and butterflies to visit his grave. For me there would be no sunflower. I would be buried in a mass-grave, where corpses would be piled on top of me. No sunflower would ever bring light into my darkness, and no butterflies would dance above my dreadful tomb….Even in death they were superior to us….[15]

Sunflower, a book in which Wiesenthal wrestled with the meaning of "forgiveness," together with other prominent thinkers and religious leaders, will have its second edition coming out soon. While absolutely sure about the idea of justice, he still seemed, after 51 years, to be searching for an answer to the question of "forgiveness." According to Jewish teaching, I learned, it is only the victim who can forgive. In a recently published biography, Wiesenthal mourned his mother, who was sent to the Belzec death camp in the summer of 1942.

Many people have lost their mother—through illness or old age, but by natural causes. Such people can bury their mother and shed tears at the funeral; they can grieve by the grave, and be close to her. The Nazis robbed me of that opportunity. My mother's grave has become a part of me…. I do not even have a photograph of my mother. When I was taken from the ghetto to the concentration camp, everything that I still possessed was taken from me…. I would give anything to have a picture of my mother.[16]

Professor Willnauer asked me if I wanted to go inside. Prodded by the serious tone of his voice, I answered yes. It was a lovely chapel with beautiful stained glass windows at both sides of the altar. "It's been a long time since the last time I was in this chapel," he said. We stood there in silence for a while. "Did you have this church during the war?" I asked. He answered, "Yes, we did. And you know what? The people in this village got together in this chapel every Sunday and prayed as if nothing was going on at the nearby hill. While thousands of human beings were murdered!"

It was at that moment that all the emotions I had somehow suppressed for the past two days since I had arrived in Austria suddenly came to the fore. I could not identify myself with the perpetrators. I could not identify myself with the victims. Yet, I could imagine myself being in this chapel, praying and not thinking about "the death hill." How easy it would have been! But, for those who perished in the Holocaust, my actions would have been just as cruel as those of the Nazis. Only after I put myself in a position of the bystanders and only after I realized how easy it would have been to become one, could I finally glimpse the deep despair the Holocaust victims must have felt. Tears, which did not come when I saw the gas chamber or the crematorium, came to my eyes.

Then I thought about Wiesenthal. I had met him again that morning just before leaving for Mauthausen. I told him that I had come back to say good bye, and we embraced each other. He told me, "Many people visit me in this office, but not a person like you." With those words, the image of the legendary Nazi hunter within me was replaced with a real human being, whose warm embrace I would never forget. One thing I had not realized until I came to Mauthausen, though, was how difficult it must have been for him to remain a human being.

Rabbi Abraham Cooper, Associate Dean of the Simon Wiesenthal Center, once told me,

> To me, Simon Wiesenthal is a miracle. I often think about the story of his refusal to give the list of the former Nazis to the Jewish partisans who came to him after the war. He knew they wanted to kill those on the list, and refused to give the list. Wiesenthal understood then that we could not live our life only through anger, even if it's righteous anger. Justice had to be restored by bringing those who had committed crimes to the court not by revenge. He understood that Cambodia was going to happen and Rwanda was going to happen unless the society would take a certain step. He knew we had to build bridges. I don't understand how he could draw that lesson in 1945. I consider it to be a miracle. But, that kind of humanity and a commitment, an incredible commitment to reconstitute the idea of justice...that is unbelievable to me.

A few days after returning from Austria, I stood in front of the Wiesenthal exhibit at the Museum of Tolerance. I looked at his picture again. A picture of Wiesenthal working at his desk—which I now know that he must still be doing in his humble office in Vienna. Gone was my previously-held image of him. Instead, I was filled with happiness of having known this remarkable human being.

NOTES

[1]Evelyn Le Chene, *Mauthausen* (London: Methuen & Co.Ltd, 1971), 190-91.

[2]Ann Frank, *The Diary of A Young Girl* (New York: Doubleday, 1995), 339.

[3]Le Chene, *Mauthausen,* 59.

[4]Simon Wiesenthal, *The Murderers Among Us* (London: Heinemann Ltd., 1967), 49.

[5]Martin Gilbert, *The Holocaust* (New York: Henry Holt and Company, 1985), 809-10.

[6]Michael Berenbaum, *The World Must Know* (New York: Little, Brown and Company, 1993), 7-8.

[7]Simon Wiesenthal , *Justice not Vengeance* (New York: Grove Weidenfeld, 1989), 28-29.

[8]Le Chene, *Mauthausen,* 60.

[9]*Simon Wiesenthal* (exhibit), Beit Hashoah- Museum of Tolerance, Los Angeles.

[10]Alan Levy, *The Wiesenthal File* (London: Constable, 1993), 349.

[11]Hella Pick, *Simon Wiesenthal* (Boston: Northeastern University Press, 1996) 311-12.

[12]*Ibid.,* 311.

[13]Levy, *The Wiesenthal File,* 57.

[14]"Nazi Hunter Warns About Populism Risks," *Los Angeles Times,* October 19, 1996.

[15]Simon Wiesenthal, *The Sunflower* (New York: Schocken Books, 1976), 20.

[16]Pick, *Wiesenthal* 32.

The Memorial Site of Mauthausen

Professor Peter Willnauer
Holocaust Teacher

Linz, a city in Upper Austria, is where Adolf Hitler spent his formative years and, under the influence of his favorite history teacher,
became "a little revolutionary."

I was to meet Professor Peter Willnauer there so he could bring
me to the memorial site of Mauthausen, the Nazi concentration camp
located near Linz. After leaving Vienna and rolling westward across
the gentle landscape of Upper Austria for two hours, the train pulled
into the old station in Linz, the city Hitler had planned to rebuild as
a future metropolis. Professor Willnauer, who teaches "how to teach
the history of the Holocaust" at the Teacher's College in Linz and
whom I had never met before, was waiting for me at the station.

I was thinking that he would find me first since it seemed that I
was the only Oriental person in the crowd. But the moment we saw
each other, both of us immediately knew we found the right person.
He seemed to be in his 50s and a very intelligent person. Rather than
a college professor, he could be a writer or a movie critic, which I
later found out he also was. "I parked my car in front of the station,
so let's walk to my car," he said in English. As we walked to his car I
explained my book project and why I wanted to visit Mauthausen.
He showed genuine interest, so I felt, in my project.

We rode in his car and headed for Mauthausen, which he said
would be about a 30 minute drive. He asked me how much of the
Holocaust history I knew about. He tried to explain the very prominent role Austria had played in the genocide of the European Jews.
He seemed to be a person who really needed to look at the other

person when he talks. He often crossed the lane unknowingly while talking to me and looking into my eyes. More than once I had to ask him to look ahead. We were lucky that not many cars were on the road to Mauthausen on that day.

"These were houses SS officers lived in with their families," he explained as we ascended the hill toward the camp site. There were neat houses along the road with a flower garden in front of each house. "They were family men, a good husband and caring father, who attended a flower garden on weekends," he told me matter-of-factly. Soon we arrived at Mauthausen, a massive fortress atop a beautiful hill. We entered a vast courtyard surrounded by medieval stone walls where, according to Professor Willnauer, newly arrived inmates had been stripped naked and told that they were not human beings any more. "Imagine thousands of inmates without clothes shivering in the winter weather in this yard," he told me. I tried and felt a chill.

During the two hours we spent at Mauthausen, he was always sensitive to my reaction to what I would see, be they pictures of piles of dead bodies, or the actual gas chamber, or the crematorium. He would ask, "Would you like to see them?" or "Would you like to go in?" I appreciated that but wanted to see everything. When we came to the gas chamber where, I was told, 150 prisoners at a time had been gassed, there were scores of high school girls inside listening to the explanation from their teacher. When I tried to join them, Professor Willnauer hesitated and said, "I can't bear the sight of innocent young people inside this chamber." It was the first instance I noticed that he himself was taking this visit very personally and emotionally. I knew that he had given many guided tours of Mauthausen to educators and students over the years. Yet, apparently he was still deeply troubled by seeing the place where hundreds of thousand of people had been killed by the Nazis more than a half century ago.

We stood in front of the brick wall against which Russian prisoners of war had been brutally executed in 1944. We did not need to exchange any words to share the horror that the wall still evoked. We had just seen the pictures of that execution.

Professor Willnauer also brought me to the quarry where prisoners had been forced to climb 186 steps of the "Death Staircase," carrying a large stone on their shoulder. I was struck by its steepness as well as by the tranquillity of the place now. We stood there looking at the staircase, from which many prisoners had fallen to their death.

On the way back to Linz we stopped at a tiny village we had seen from Mauthausen. Professor Willnauer told me that he had grown up there during the war. He showed me the church he had attended and the kindergarten he had gone to. Inside the church he said, "It's been a long time since the last time I was in this church." For both of us, it was an emotional moment. Dusk was beginning to settle inside the quiet chapel.

Back in his car, we resumed our conversation. I learned that he had been very active in teaching the history of the Holocaust, especially about Austria's involvement for the last twenty years. "Wasn't it difficult in those days, though?" I asked. "When I started, yes, it was very difficult to talk about our country's role in the Holocaust. But for the last five years or so, I began to receive a lot of support from my colleagues and my students." Then he said, "Teaching in the classroom is all right. But every time I visit Mauthausen I tell myself that this is going to be the last time I come here. It's too painful." I did not know what to say. He had just spent long hours at Mauthausen with me. Did he mean to say that was painful for him? He must have realized how I felt from my silence. He said, "But I am glad I could give you a tour today." Then he said a truly remarkable thing. "When I teach the Holocaust, I want my students to see my inner struggle. How I am struggling to come to terms with that horrible event at a very personal level...." It was my turn to gaze at his face.

When we arrived in Linz, I had almost an hour before my train for Vienna would leave. We decided to have coffee together. Having settled in a small cafe in the station, I asked the question that had kept coming back ever since we were in front of the gas chamber at Mauthausen. "You don't have to answer, but was your father a Nazi?" Professor Willnauer looked at me straight in the eyes and said, "Yes, a very devoted one, I heard." "You heard? You didn't know your father?" "No, my mother remarried right after the war. My earliest memory was with my stepfather." "But didn't you ask your mother about your real father?" "No, never. My stepfather was a very abusive person. I really didn't have a happy child life. You see, I was always angry at my mother. How did she end up raising me in such a terrible condition? I rebelled against her all the time until her death. I never asked her about my real father."

I could not bring myself to ask if his father was stationed at Mauthausen. His mother was from the village at the foot of Mauthausen and he was born in 1940. It was the only logical conclusion that his father must have worked at the camp. Was he executed after the war or did he escape to somewhere? I just swallowed all those questions. I remembered our conversation in front of the pictures of the Nazi officers at the exhibit hall of Mauthausen. "Some of these officers look so young. They must have been in their 20s!" "Yes, and they were often the most cruel ones." What went through his mind when he said that?

He asked me if it was all right for him to smoke, to which I said yes. He lit a cigarette and smoked. I was beginning to worry that I had asked too personal questions and that he had considered me rude. After all, he was kind enough to give me a half day tour. The last thing I should do was to be rude to him. So, I was not prepared to absorb his next words. "Do you know why I have to do what I am doing—teaching young people about the true history of the Holocaust?

Because this is the only way to purify my blood, murderous blood, flowing within me." Being a captive audience, I could tell that those words did not come easily for him.

The force of his emotion and his honesty overwhelmed me. I had to restrain myself from holding his hand on the table. All I could say was, "I think you are a very courageous person to do that."

We spent the last few minutes talking about our families. He showed me pictures of his wife and two adult daughters and I reciprocated with pictures of my family. And soon, it was time for me to go. When we got to the platform we asked a stranger to take a picture of us. Standing beside me he said, "This is the very first time I take a picture of myself at Linz station." "I will send it to you," I answered.

With one bright flash from my camera, my trip to Linz came to an end. It was only six hours earlier that I had set foot in this city, a totally strange place, and now I was leaving with so many memories. People started boarding the train for Vienna that had just arrived. As we shook hands I said, "Thank you very much, Professor Willnauer." I was thinking that I would probably never see him again. He kissed me on the cheek and said, "Good bye. You have to get on the train now."

Sitting alone on the night train to Vienna was, perhaps, what I needed most at that time. I had arrived in Austria two days earlier and was leaving the very next morning. I hardly did any sightseeing in Vienna. All I did was meeting people, the most remarkable people I had ever met, and visiting places where I felt emotions I had never felt before. All the memories and all the emotions finally began to sink within me as I closed my eyes and let myself be carried away by steady motion of the moving train.

---

* I later learned through my telephone conversation with Professor Willnauer that his father had not worked at Mauthausen. Yet, he kindly allowed me to include this essay in this book.

Being True to History and to Oneself

Raoul Hilberg
Professor emeritus of political science
The University of Vermont

The Destruction of the European Jews was the book I should read and its author, Raoul Hilberg, was the person I should interview. That was my conclusion by the fall of 1996. Everywhere I turned for suggested reading in the study of the Holocaust, the subject on which close to two thousand books have been written,[1] this title and his name appeared at the top of the list. Praise was abundant. "The product of painstaking and wide-ranging research, Hilberg's book offers a magisterial synthesis on a scale that no one has matched before or since."[2] "...arguably the single most important book about the Holocaust."[3]

Hilberg was born in Vienna in 1926 to Jewish parents who emigrated to the United States in 1939. As a youth he saw the rise of the Third Reich, and witnessed its fall as a young American soldier. He was a member of the War Documentation Project where he examined masses of German records in their original folders.

Hilberg began his work on *The Destruction of the European Jews* in 1948 and finally published it in 1961. Using German documentation as his major source, since he believed that only the perpetrators had the over view, he described "the vast organization of the Nazi machinery of destruction and the men who performed important functions in this machine."[4]

Although he had stated from the outset that this was not a book about the Jews and that it was a book about the people who destroyed the Jews,[5] the book was highly controversial because of his statement that the passivity and the cooperation by Jews to the Nazis

57

contributed to their own destruction. He faced a firestorm of criticism. Some declared that his conclusion was "defaming the dead"[6] and that nothing was learned from blaming the catastrophe on its victims.[7] One Jewish historian attacked him for not being familiar with Jewish history or Jewish traditional life and culture.[8]

He described the campaign against him since the book was first published as "a thirty-year war."[9] In his recent autobiography Hilberg wrote, "in my research and writing I was pursuing not merely another direction but one which was the exact opposite of a signal that pulsated endlessly through the Jewish community."[10] How could a historian who was considered the dean of Holocaust study be subjected to such vicious criticism for such a long time? And why was it so important for him that he be driven by the "sheer force of logic" in his examination of Jewish behavior? My interest in him grew. Watching the acclaimed French documentary *Shoah*, where Hilberg appeared as a masterful commentator, only increased my determination to meet him. I summoned my courage to write him a letter asking for an interview. Within a few days he wrote me back saying that he would be delighted to meet with me.

So, it was on a late autumn day of 1996 that I boarded a 16-seat airplane at the La Guardia airport in New York where I had flown in from Los Angeles overnight. As the airplane approached Burlington, VT, where Professor Hilberg had lived for the last forty years, I was mildly struck by the smallness and loneliness of the town I saw down below. However, when I stood at the front door of his home I had an unexplainable feeling that I would have a very good interview. So, I knocked on the door....

What was it that inspired you to write about the destruction of the European Jews?

I had my college training interrupted by the war. After I came back from Europe, I took a course titled "The Rise of the National State" at Brooklyn College. It was taught by Professor Hans Rosenberg and the subject was the history of bureaucracy in England, France and Germany. His cutoff period was from 1660 to 1930. One day he mentioned that the Napoleonic invasion of Spain produced atrocities, the likes of which had not happened since. To me there was a set of overtones here, of pushing aside of the whole Nazi regime. By the way, Rosenberg himself was a Jew. So I raised my hand. I wasn't exactly bashful and said, "What do you call six million dead Jews?" He started saying, "Well, that was very complicated…." And without really answering my question he went back to the subject of the course. The whole incident took but a minute. Now I think that was a turning point because I started to think if Rosenberg could make a comment like that in 1947 in the City of New York, something was drastically, drastically wrong, something had been suppressed.

So you sensed that he was avoiding the subject?

Not only was he avoiding it, everyone was avoiding it. He would not have been able to make that statement, he would have been challenged by the entire class if the subject had been out, if people were conscious of it. Don't forget in 1947 everything was past.

But it had been only two years since the end of WWII.

Yes, but two things were happening. First of all it became evident that we were going to have problems with the Soviet Union. The beginning of the Cold War. So, we were already talking about rearming of Germany…

But that was for politicians, what about scholars?

Well, my whole discovery, you see, was that scholars were not immune. They follow the politicians. That I became aware of even in high school. I was aware of the fact that scholarly writing in the fields of political science, economics or history was always influenced by politics. I took it for granted. Here we were turning Germany around, you know, not that we welcomed Germany but we needed them in order to deal with the Russians. So it wasn't really that we were denying the past, but we had to put it behind us.

So you felt that if you were not going to write about it nobody would. Was that your feeling?

That's right. I believed it. I was 22 years old at that time and I really believed it. And I was actually right. Nobody would write about it using German documents in this country.

Was it because of the political pressure at that time or the enormity of the task?

Enormity of the task won't stop certain people, especially if they are young and don't know what they are tackling. But the political issue was something else, I mean, as soon as I came to my sponsor, professor Franz Neumann, with my outline for a doctoral dissertation entitled *"The Destruction of the European Jews"* he said, "This is your funeral."

How did you feel when you heard those words?

Well, it was very sobering because I knew immediately what it would mean. Although I had my dream of ending up in some kind of professorship somewhere, that topic would kill me and it did! No question about it.

Yet, you were not discouraged?

No, I was not discouraged because I had a characteristic of going alone. I was an only child and I spent a lot of time in my mind alone. I was a bachelor until the age of 38. So, somehow the prospect of not being able to achieve a certain normal goal in the academic world did not deter me although it was a serious matter because not having been born in the U.S., I was not eligible for certain government jobs. Rather, I felt an outrage in every direction, be it in the Jewish community, be it in America, in Germany, be it in every place, you know…. "Are you going to bury this? You would forget something that you do not even know and understand?" It's illogical. Although politically and psychologically forgetting would make sense, logic and psychology are two different things. And remember there was discrimination against Jews in those days. For example, there was a movie called "Night and Fog" in which Jews were not mentioned. So the notion was "yes it happened," but the victims were not identified. It was bizarre to me because, of course, the definition of who was to be killed was crucial and a cornerstone of the whole process. You could say that I was protesting, my whole life and my whole work were protests.

How about the survivors? Didn't they want to tell?

They were ignored. That's true even for the most famous survivors. In fact, when Elie Wiesel's fantastic story of his first book "Night" came out here, it was no best seller.

So you knew what kind of reaction you would get?

Yes, because I talked to many survivors. They were told to forget it no matter where they went—Palestine, the United States or Paris, they were told to forget it. And it was not unusual. Every soldier, he may have fought in the Battle of the Bulge or he may have been on Omaha beach, received the same message—forget the past and get on with their life.

But you must have had some hope that someday your work would be appreciated, otherwise how could you keep going?

Well yes, I had a hope, more than a hope. I had, perhaps, an unjustified expectation. One of the reasons that I was constantly aware of the need to write appropriately to the subject was that if I were not writing in a proper style it would not last.

You mean being objective?

Yes, it had to be objective and had to be clear so that it would be understood a hundred years from now and it would be understood in a different country.

Did you really think that far into the future?

Of course. I grew up in a home where my parents kept classic books in bookshelves. Well, if I were not writing a book worthy of sitting with these books, why bother?

So here you were in your early 20s, and you were thinking about writing a book that someday would be a classic. But did you anticipate that it would take 13 years for you to complete?

Oh, no, I gave it 5 years. I did think it would be a 500-page book, but in the end it was an 800-page double-column book, an equivalent of a 1000-page book.

You wrote recently in your memoir that in your life you had always wanted the truth about yourself. I was very touched by that statement. You had to write about the Jewish cooperation in their destruction process because that was a historical truth you had found. And if you had not written about it you would not have been true to yourself. I think Japanese people in general are not raised or trained to learn the importance of facing historical truth. Maybe it has something to do with the Japanese tradition of group orientation. It seems that the truth always belongs to a group rather than an individual. It is no wonder then that in Japan historical truth, or for that matter any truth, can be changed or manipulated depending on the group. Where does it come from? Your being true to yourself.

Well, it comes from the culture I grew up in. And I always hate pretense.

But being true to yourself is not always easy is it? I brought an article which I am sure you have read. In this "Commentary" article, Lucy Dawidowicz was quoted to have said, "Nobody can write a genuine Jewish history unless you love the Jewish people." She seemed to care more about historians' loyalty to the subject than their being objective.

Yes, yes, yes, I read that article. Actually my father had a very similar view. He felt for a long time that I should not touch the subject. I was not committed the way he thought I should be to Jewish community or identified with it. So, yes just as I cut myself off from people, being a loner, I cut myself off from the Jewish community also. It would be a fair question to say, okay, suppose I can't love, suppose I can't love a bunch of people, suppose I can't love a nation and suppose I can't love the world, so what? so that means I can't look at it?

The reason I ask this question is that I recently read an article in a Japanese magazine which argued that if we teach our children about the rape of Nanking or the comfort women, they won't love Japan any more. The

author was suggesting that the study of history must serve some purpose,
like making young people proud of their country. Well, I am not sure that
should be a part of the reason young people study history. Then, where is
historical truth? What about being true to oneself?

Well, I can talk about the prevailing attitude of the Jewish community. That is, okay whatever I said about the truth is very
welcome, very useful and very necessary, only I shouldn't have
dealt with the Jews at all. I should have left them out if I couldn't
say some nice things about them. Nobody should say anything
unless you were there or you love the Jewish people. Otherwise
you shouldn't have said it. My attitude is, wait a minute, that is a
whole meaning of objectivity. If the Germans didn't have personnel, and they sure didn't, to carry this process to a conclusion
without Jewish cooperation, I've got to make that statement.

Because it was a historical truth?

Oh yes. And I knew then, and I know now that the next generation that will not see any survivors, because all survivors will be
dead, that generation will not mind hearing those. It is already
happening. This year, two diaries have been published here. One
is a diary of a Jewish policeman in a small ghetto who was involved in rounding up Jewish people. I don't think it could have
been published 20 years ago, no way. Another diary was that of a
teenager who lived in a larger ghetto. He wrote that he had to
buy the ration no matter how small it was. Now, in a community
like Jew's where they are supposed to have a communal responsibility and it turned out that communal responsibility had a very
severe limit. Now, that kind of story was not very welcome. How
can you love people when you are left on a street to starve to
death? This kind of book would not have been published 20
years ago. I will go so far as to say because you brought up Lucy,
who is now dead, that there are some taboos in Holocaust studies. Virtually all of these taboos deal with Jews' reactions or Jewish behaviors. And these taboos will still exist so long as survivors
are still alive. But when they are gone the taboos will be gone.

You seem to be saying that the Japanese, too, have to wait. But the prob-

lem is that we didn't have a person like you in Japan. It is only recent that Japan's general population openly talks about such issues the biological experiments by the Japanese Imperial Army in Manchuria or the comfort women.

Chinese writers may be able to write about them, but I think they should be written by Japanese historians using the Japanese documents to be truly objective. Well, most countries don't face their history squarely. When archives were opened all of a sudden in the former Soviet Union, The Russians found out about the Gulag and now they have to live with that past. Or take France, it was a divided country of collaborators, resisters and of course a lot of people in the middle, and they have to live with that past. And the way to live with it is often just not talking about it. So, many countries bury some part of their histories, and the only difference is the degree to which each country does that. The United States does that, too. For example, I have a problem with our dropping of the Atomic bombs.

Have you written about it?

No, but I have talked a lot about it in my classes. I am convinced that they were unnecessary. And this is the issue that the United States has never faced, never. So, everybody has a dark history. Then what's so special about Germans? I think the one special thing about Germans is that they planed and delivered the destruction of the European Jews, women and children without an exception, after the war was definitely decided. They carried them through. We can't explain it, and we can't understand it. But it is different from what we Americans did, Japanese did or other nations did. It is different in its conception and in its massiveness and in its relentlessness. The Holocaust was different and unprecedented. It was a complete, massive detailed undertaking that required utilization of all of the organized German society.

Since it was so unique you don't think it can happen again? Or do you think if all the elements of the Holocaust appear again sometime, somewhere in some country, it can happen again?

That's a key question and I cannot answer it. If you think that only Germans were capable of it then you are optimistic, but if you think anyone in the same circumstances is also capable of it then you are very pessimistic. That's the only thing I can answer.

The only difference, though, is if it ever happens again it would be the second time.

Yes, it would. And that is a major difference because, in a certain sense, what makes the second time is the knowledge of the first time.

Are you saying that the second time is more likely?

Wow, another unanswerable question! Yes, in a way I wrote a technical manual for destruction of the Jewish people. But I also wrote a chapter at the very end which I feel is of some importance. But the fact that it was totally ignored also is significant. I wrote that we had discriminatory systems in America. Well that was true when I was writing this book in the 40's and 50's. How do you end discriminations? Now you use the same steps but you go in reverse. First of all, if you want to do something for minorities de-concentrate them, let them live among us. Give them housing then they can get a job and then they can get a set of group identifications with a larger role.

My last question to you. In your memoir you wrote that Mr. Claude Lanzmann, the producer of the French documentary Shoah, *had said to you, "You were Czerniakow." Adam Czerniakow was chairman of the Jewish Council of the Warsaw ghetto who kept a diary during the war. The Jewish councils were the organized leadership of the Jewish communities which the Germans depended on in carrying out their final solution. What did Mr. Lanzmann mean when he said that you were Czerniakow?*

When I discovered that diary in Jerusalem in 1968 I was immediately interested. Well, Czerniakow was a typical bureaucrat, the mind set, not big thinking but trying to solve this little problem and that little problem. I didn't expect to identify with Czerniakow.

With yourself?

Yes, I mean, to see myself in his place to sort of follow his thoughts in his daily life. He was about 59 when the war broke out and I was about that age, maybe a little younger, when I started reading his diary. So I could already identify with his age. He had a sense of irony. One thing that struck me most about is that he had an open eye, he did not fool himself or kid himself. He really expected things to get worse and worse. But he was attached to the idea of honor. My father who served in WWI used to talk about honor although he thought the war was preposterous. Czerniakow could have left, but he didn't. He also knew that he would fail.

Failure means that he could not save the Jewish people. Then why did he serve?

Someone had to. He didn't believe in resistance, he didn't see the possibility. But as long as he could have people just survive one day to the next, he gambled. He gambled with dying patients. It was the same situation in which Japan was placed in 1941. Japan had no oil and was a dying patient, so Japan had to gamble. And there was also a sense of honor. Czerniakow didn't expect to win either, but there was a wall around the ghetto just as Japan was encroached. And when he failed he committed suicide. He committed suicide after it became clear that he could not save the orphans from deportation.

Did he know that the deportation meant the death camp?

I think he heard the rumors. He must have drawn a conclusion. And I identify with him.

This is his last entry which precedes his death by only a few hours, and which Mr. Lanzmann had you read on camera. "It is three o'clock. So far four thousand are ready to go. The orders are that there must be nine thousand by four o'clock." This is the man who was placed in the position of facilitating the Jewish cooperation in their own destruction—the topic for which you had to fight for thirty years. Then, what is it that makes you identify with him?

His clear-sightedness, and a sense of honor.

After talking for almost three hours, we realized that the sun had long set and the night fell upon his beloved backyard where, he wrote in his memoir, "gradually, almost imperceptibly, the decades rolled away."[11] We decided to go out for dinner. He called a cab and we went to a charming restaurant in town. Our conversation did not confine itself to the Holocaust any more. We talked about our children, his best friend and his being an atheist. We kept talking until he, knowing that I had not slept almost 24 hours, finally said, "I will walk you to your hotel before you collapse."

Although the temperature was in the 30s, the night was beautiful and the air was crisp. We kept talking as we walked. I learned that he had been a very tough teacher at the University of Vermont, but he did not miss teaching since he had retired a few years earlier. He pointed to the bookstore across the street which he claimed had the largest inventory in the East Coast. He laughed when I responded, "But why here?"

When we arrived at the hotel where I was staying, I asked him if he wanted me to call a cab for him. He answered no, adding, "I always walk. I love walking." I was not convinced. "But it's cold." "I'm used to it." "How long will it take for you to walk home?" "Well, perhaps an hour." "Oh, please, let me call a cab." No, he was not going to listen to me. He shook my hand and wished me good luck on my book project. And he walked away into the night.

Back in my room, I was totally exhausted, yet I could not sleep thinking about him walking at that very moment. "I should have insisted to call a cab," I thought. The image of him walking alone in the dark did not leave me for a while. I asked myself, "After all, isn't that what he has been doing all those years? Walking alone on a dark road without guiding lights...."

Then, I thought about his words during the interview—"Suppose I can't love, suppose I can't love a bunch of people, suppose I can't love a nation and suppose I can't love the world, so what? So that means I can't look at it?" Why did you say that, Professor Hilberg? I had expected that you would say, "I love Jewish people and care about them in my own way. That's why I wrote my book." But you did not say that. Was it because you were never allowed to say that?

Or did it mean you had been hurt so much and for so long? I did not know why. All I knew was that you were a warm, honest and caring human being with a deep sense of honor. And although it was only a short distance, I shall always cherish the memory of having a walk with you.

A few weeks later, I received a thank you card from Professor Hilberg. In addition to thanking me for the pictures I had sent him, which we had taken together in front of his house, he wrote, "The few hours you spent here was my pleasure."

NOTES

[1]Michael Marrus, *The Holocaust in History* (New York: Meridian Book, 1987), 6.

[2]*Ibid.*, 48.

[3]John Roth and Michael Berenbaum ed. *Holocaust: Religious & Philosophical Implications* (New York: Paragon House, 1989), 115.

[4]Raoul Hilberg, *The Destruction of The European Jews* (Chicago: Quadrangle Books, 1961), V.

[5]*Ibid.*

[6]Oscar Handlin, "Jewish Resistance to the Nazis," *Commentary*, November 1962, 399.

[7]*Ibid.*, 405.

[8]Lucy Dawidowicz, *The Holocaust and the Historians* (Cambridge: Harvard University Press, 1981),178.n16.

[9]Raoul Hilberg, *The Politics of Memory* (Chicago: Ivan R. Dee, 1996), 129.

[10]*Ibid.*, 128.

[11]Hilberg, *The Politics of Memory*, 165.

---

* Professor Hilberg's words are taken from our tape-recorded conversation, which took place in the natural setting, without editing.

Jews Did Fight Back

Dr. Neil C. Sandberg
Founding Director and Consultant
Asia and Pacific Rim Institute of
The American Jewish Committee

In 1942, 17-year-old Neil Sandberg was ready to fight against the Nazis in Europe. He volunteered to join the Navy intending to fight and even die for the people his mother had left behind in Poland three decades earlier. He was sent to the Pacific instead while the entire family of his mother were killed in the Holocaust. He still remembers her reaction—screaming in Yiddish, "All dead!"—when that terrible news reached them after the war.

Learning what had happened in the Holocaust in greater detail, and the pain and suffering of his people, made him decide to become actively involved in the organized Jewish community. Since 1950, he has been working for the American Jewish Committee, especially promoting outreach programs to people of other cultures. To encourage mutual understanding and respect among people, he also taught at universities and wrote several social science text books.

After serving as AJC's Western Regional Director for many years, Dr. Sandberg became the founding director of the Asia and Pacific Rim Institute, an organization created by the American Jewish Committee in 1989 to enhance understanding and strengthen ties between the Jewish people and Asian countries including Japan. He wrote in 1990, "One of the underlying realities is that there has been limited personal contact between the Japanese and the Jewish people.... What have been lacking are the vehicles through which positive information about the Jews and Judaism could be made available in Japan." [1]

It was based on this belief that personal contact had to be established between the Japanese and the Jewish people that Dr. Sandberg visited Japan many times to conduct dialogues with government officials, journalists, scholars and many others.

As I sought his advice on this book project from time to time, we became close friends. The mere fact that he has been working for a Jewish organization longer than my entire life gave me a sense of humility, yet he was always willing to let me reach my own conclusions. He was incredibly patient in making sure that I saw issues from more than one perspective.

I once asked him if he could find in his organization's archives a 35-year-old article which I needed to read to prepare myself for Professor Raul Hilberg's chapter. The article, "Jewish Resistance to the Nazis," which appeared in the American Jewish Committee's *Commentary* magazine in 1962 and was written by Harvard history professor Oscar Handlin, was the first major rebuttal to Professor Hilberg's *The Destruction of the European Jews.*

Dr. Sandberg, with his typical graciousness, retrieved the article and made a copy for me. Also with his typical self-restraint, he did not make any comment either on the article or on the book while I was writing about Professor Hilberg. He did tell me, however, that if I wanted to hear about his thoughts on Jewish resistance during the Holocaust, he would be glad to share them with me.

It was long after I had finished writing Professor Hilberg's chapter that Dr. Sandberg and I finally sat down to discuss the issue of Jewish resistance and his longtime involvement in promoting mutual understanding between the Jewish people and the Japanese people.

How has the Jewish community coped with the notion of Jewish passivity during the Holocaust?

> Some of us felt that this view was not completely accurate and that there was a tradition of resistance in the Jewish experience. We have argued that during the Holocaust, despite terribly difficult conditions, Jews did fight back to save themselves and their

families, that there was a significant record of mutual aid and assistance and that this history was not fully told.

It was, to some extent, for that reason that the American Jewish Committee collaborated with Professor Yehuda Bauer of Hebrew University in Israel and asked him to work with us in producing a publication that would describe Jewish resistance during the Nazi Holocaust. We thought it was important to tell that story to more people so that Jews would have a greater understanding of what actually took place and be able to place themselves in the context of those events in a way that would sustain their self-regard. Bauer did that study for us and it was published as a pamphlet some 30 years ago and distributed widely in the Jewish community, the non-Jewish community, and the media.

What did that study find?

The works of Yehuda Bauer and others, including one of our longtime staff people Lucy Dawidowicz who wrote a book called *The War Against The Jews*, were, to some extent, a response to Hilberg's approach. Professor Hilberg took his data from the archives of the Nazis. He told the story, in a sense, through the eyes of the perpetrators of the Holocaust. Germans were very efficient in keeping their records and Hilberg used their information brilliantly. But in describing this experience through the perspective of the Nazis he may have presented a view of the Jewish people that was pejorative. The Nazis wanted to destroy all of the Jewish people and succeeded in killing six million Jews. They had a very negative and hostile view of Jews and their contributions to society and world culture. They saw them as a despised and satanic people who deserved to die.

Yehuda Bauer and other scholars who tried to round out the picture and add other dimensions to this analysis sought to portray the Jews in a way that I believe was somewhat more perceptive. They looked at resistance not only as carrying a rifle and shooting Germans, but looked at it in a much broader way. They looked at it as armed resistance and as unarmed resistance—the ability and willingness of people to take great risks in various ways to stay alive and defend themselves and their families.

That armed resistance took place is clear. There was resistance in several major ghettoes, such as the Warsaw ghetto, the Vilna ghetto, and other centers of Jewish life. There were rebellions in the death camps themselves where Jews, out of a sense of desperation and realizing they were going to be killed, used sticks and their hands in order to fight back knowing they would die, but at least feeling a sense of satisfaction in fighting against the evils of Nazi terror.

It is true that for many centuries Jews were a passive people who believed in study, in learning, and in discussion. It is not unlike the Japanese tradition where people respect a passive and reflective approach to life. In order to survive, Jews learned those skills—including how to avoid conflict and confrontation. But the tragedy is that during the Holocaust, even when there was resistance by Jews they were really powerless. They had no guns or weapons with which to defend themselves.

The notion of resistance really has to be looked at in various ways. Jews, when they tried to fight back, when they escaped from the ghettoes into the forests and tried to join the partisan groups in Poland and in parts of Russia, were often denied the opportunity to cooperate with these groups because they were Jews. There was so much hostility and so much anti-Semitism among the local populations.

I would also say that the other type of resistance, unarmed resistance, was especially significant. When Jews had to sneak food into the ghettoes where they were starving, that was an act of resistance. If you were caught you would be killed by the Nazis. In keeping with the tradition of the Jewish people of learning and education, we organized schools. We educated our children even in the ghettoes where people were starving and dying of diseases and killed randomly by barbaric soldiers. Still, every day children would learn their lessons, they would learn to read and they would learn the history and religion of the Jewish people. There were many underground newspapers and this illustrates the different kinds of resistance of a people who refused to die and who hoped for the best, as they sought to survive in hostile environments.

Can you imagine living in a society where you are hated and despised, where no one is interested in your ideas and beliefs, and where you are in constant danger of being physically attacked? This is what Jews had to contend with, being among hate-filled people like the Nazis as well as antagonistic local populations. They knew that no one would care if they came under attack. In these circumstances, it is understandable that Jews felt a profound sense of helplessness. And yet they maintained their dignity and their faith. Many of them tried to resist, even while suspecting that it might not change the terrible outcome that awaited most of the Jews in Europe. So there was resistance. I would argue and others who have done statistical analyses would argue that the percentage of Jews who did end up fighting as partisans and in other ways was even greater than that of the indigenous populations of the countries in which Jews lived.

Have you thought about how you would have acted if you had lived in Europe in those days?

I would have been 14 years old in 1939 and 16 or 17 when the Holocaust was being carried out in its most criminal way. I was young enough, strong enough, and brash enough to believe that I would have made an attempt to join a group and fight back. At the same time I would have felt a sense of obligation to my family. And to leave my mother and my grandparents to die without staying to help them would have caused a serious personal conflict. So, I would have had to make a difficult choice.

It should be said that whether resistance was armed or unarmed, in most cases it did not really change the outcome. That is an important point. The Nazis were not brought down by partisans, they were brought down by Allied invasions—tanks, planes, and bombs and the destruction of massive numbers of troops and weapons through the coordinated efforts of many nations. Internal resistance generally hindered but did not change the results of German invasion and Nazi brutality. The destruction of the Jewish population would have taken place in any event because so few people or nations were willing to help save the Jews. The Nazis were diabolically clever as they created a mass psychology of deception that lured many Jews into the death camps. The Jews were told that they were being deported to work, not to be slaughtered. Some people arriving at the camps were given postcards to send back to their friends and relatives, saying things were all right in the camps. And after they finished writing the cards, they were put to death. For a long time, Jews believed, they wanted to believe, that they and their children would survive if only they cooperated with the Nazis. As we look back at these circumstances, we might say they were naive or even foolish. Yet at the time, living in a culture where they had no power, and where they had been persecuted for centuries, it is understandable that only a fraction of the Jewish population had the wherewithal to fight back. But many Jews did resist along with other people in places where the Nazis and their local collaborators maintained deadly control.

What did the experience of Jewish resistance during the Holocaust, or lack of it depending on the differing views, teach the post-war Jewish population?

Some would say that Jews have learned to transcend two thousand years of relative powerlessness and passivity in order to defend themselves in the modern age. We were able to move quickly from a long and difficult history highlighted by prejudice and persecution in Europe to become a new kind of Jew who would be a fighter willing to die for his country and his people. Much of this happened in a very short time from the period leading up to 1945 when the last Jew was killed in Europe to 1948 when the state of Israel was created.

Today, most Israeli Jews, men and women, serve in their armed forces willingly. Never again will they be put in a position of having to give up their lives without being able to fight back effectively. They all know that they have to resist their enemies or die, and they have chosen to live. They have learned from the tragedy of the Holocaust. Most of them have grown up in a culture in which they are not despised and humiliated because of who they are, but are accepted and respected for their unique qualities, their intelligence, their family and group loyalty, a commitment to justice, and an interest in the well being of not only their own people but of others. Much of this happened in only a few years so that the Jews of Europe who were the victims now should be seen as the same Jews we see in Israel and elsewhere today. They are determined to control their own destiny and are no longer content to place their fate in the hands of others.

It seems to me that your work in the last forty or fifty years has been also a resistance, perhaps in a very peaceful and enlightening way—promoting better understanding of who you were among the Jewish people on the one hand, and reaching out to other groups of people to enhance mutual understanding on the other. Was it easy for you to reach out to different groups of people?

As a Jew I did not have much choice. We are such a small group and we were relatively powerless for so long that we had to learn how to change the rules of intergroup and intercultural relations. We had to learn how to develop alliances and coalitions with people of different backgrounds in order to be more effective in the political arena and in world culture. So getting along with others is the basic rule in Jewish life. Without that, representing about two percent of the U.S. population, we would not have any serious impact. But having friends among many other groups in society with similar values and points of view, as well as similar interests, we are more influential and more effective in expressing our concerns. We have learned that we have to create an environment of intergroup cooperation in order to have a political impact on society.

Since 1989, you have been especially involved in promoting mutual understanding between the Japanese people and your people. Drawing on your longtime experience in this country, what would you tell the Japanese people about such issues as pluralism?

One of the ideas that we have discussed with a number of Japanese leaders is the extent to which the experience of American cultural groups in adjusting to the diverse segments of society is applicable to Japan or Asia. Japan likes to see itself as a homogenous society. But there are now recognized minorities in Japan including the Koreans, the Ainu, and the Burakumin. There are different social class groups and there are regional differences. Indeed, Japan is actually a very complex and diverse society. That is why some of us who've been working with Japan about anti-Semitism and other issues feel that we may have something to contribute to Japanese understanding of the ways in which we deal with such issues. We have trained ourselves, we've studied in universities, we've done research, we've written books, we've been practitioners working in this country and all over the world in dealing with issues of conflict between people and groups, as well as the amelioration of such conflict.

There is a growing body of people in Japan, still small but increasing, who have come to the realization that Japan cannot live isolated within and accepted without. As Japan moves into the larger world, it has to engage culturally with everybody else. The Japanese cannot be bigoted within Japan and good guys in the rest of the world because the media tells the rest of the world about what happens in Japan. So if there is prejudice against African Americans in Japan, like people having Black Sambo dolls that offend African Americans, leaders of black organizations and elected officials in the U.S. are offended. If the Japanese want to be friendly with the United States and accepted by the American people, they have to understand that their actions at home impact their image in the world. And they are beginning to accept this new reality. Certainly, there are many people in the government who understand the nature of the problem and are willing to act on it.

I remember meeting here in Los Angeles some years ago with the Dalai Lama and a group of leaders from various religious groups. He expressed his admiration for us because of our ability to communicate across racial, religious, and even socioeconomic lines and to find areas in which we could express our mutual understanding, and collaborate on projects for the benefit of all. He admired the pluralism of America. In the discussion period I asked him about whether or not this experience was possibly applicable to Asia where each nation has a strong and separate national tradition. I don't think he had given this a lot of thought and he responded that it would be very difficult. I don't believe he meant this as a negative answer. And so we are starting to see in some Japanese universities studies of other cultures and efforts made by government, in the media and by business to use American cross-cultural approaches because we have been among the pioneers in this area.

After having dialogues with many Japanese and having worked with them on many occasions, what is your feeling toward the Japanese people today?

When I started meeting with Japanese people, instinctively I felt a sense of kinship. What I am about to say shouldn't be misunderstood. Today, I don't look at Japanese people as Japanese. When I am in Tokyo walking around the Ginza or anyplace else and I see all these people, I am now at the point where I look for the human being, the individual person and not their group characteristics. That applies here too. I don't look at Japanese men and women generally as members of a certain group. Sure, I am aware of it when we discuss our histories, our educational backgrounds and how we came to be who we are and what we are. But as a person I am not particularly aware of that. I don't see that in you. I don't see you as a Japanese woman. I see you as an interesting person who asks provocative questions and tries to elicit responses from me and from others on a subject about which I care deeply. So I think to that extent we have transcended group identification making it more a matter of individual identity.

For many Japanese, though, the Jewish people are still a mystery. While we are amazed by the long history of survival by your people, at the same time we are mystified as to what has kept your people who you are for such a long time without having a geographical place of your own. Unfortunately, this sense of mystery often prevents us Japanese from seeing Jewish people as our fellow human beings. Any thoughts on this?

Most Jews accept the notion that they will always survive as a people. Indeed, our tradition and teachings tell us that we have an obligation to survive. Still, you have to understand that there are very few Jews in the world. We are not talking about a massive population like in China or India or even Japan. We are talking about 13 or 14 million Jews living dispersed in the entire world. One third of the Jewish population was destroyed by the Nazis and they were never replaced. Our birth rates are very low, so today we have a very limited population. Nonetheless, this small Jewish group is very visible, and has contributed many of the great ideas and ideals as their unique contribution to civilization, including the notion of human equality and a belief in a monotheistic God. Despite their small numbers, Jews are heavily involved in the intellectual, cultural, and professional spheres, and are prominent in the physical and social sciences, literature, law and medicine. Jewish artists and musicians are also in abundance, but they are usually identified by the media as Americans or as Europeans rather than as Jews. Consequently, the Japanese people are often unaware of their Jewishness. It is generally when Jews are portrayed in an anti-Semitic way that this identity rises to public consciousness. This negative image of Jews has to be examined carefully because it can be quite destructive as we saw in the Holocaust. This is done very effectively in a recent book called *Jews in the Japanese Mind* written by Professors David G. Goodman and Masanori Miyazawa.

We are anxious to convey to the people of Japan that being

Jewish means having a set of values and a special outlook on God, man, and the world. Jews are held together by their common memories, history, religion, and the struggle against persecution, as well as by the feeling that being Jewish has meaning and purpose. Jewish survival and renewal is manifested for each individual through personal honesty, compassion, and advocacy of justice and mercy. The survival of Jewish civilization ultimately depends on our belief in a shared destiny and a messianic ingredient in which Jews seek a more perfect world and a place in achieving it.

In a book you published in the late 70's, you wrote about the difficulty people had to understand and to accept those who came from different backgrounds. What do you think has to happen before Japanese people can see Jewish people, or any other group of people for that matter, as individual human beings rather than as members of a certain group?

We see a great deal of evidence in the world today that people still cling to their group identities. Many of us have strong feelings of national pride that bind us together to reinforce our common histories and traditions. There are also religious, cultural and social institutions that act as a kind of glue to tie us to one another in a group framework. These can be very positive as they provide social and psychological support for the individual.

At the same time, we observe some of the negative aspects of tribalism, for example the ethnic cleansing so tragically prevalent in places like Bosnia and Rwanda. And here in the U.S. we have many different racial and ethnic groups, so that overcoming intergroup conflict is essential. One of the important aspects of this effort is dealing with stereotypes through which we tend to overgeneralize about individuals by unjustified and irrational attributions solely based on their membership in particular racial, ethnic or religious groups. This is often a negative response that is reflected in our attitudes toward others.

In the social sciences, we've learned that it is easier to change behavior than attitudes, but they are usually associated with each other. You can change behavior by adopting a law like saying that you can't go through a red light. And if you break this law you will be punished. In the case of cultural prejudice we now have hate crimes laws. If you attack a person who is Japanese American because you don't like his background, it is not only against the law that you hit him physically, but an associated aspect of punishment relates to the cultural bias that motivated the act. We believe that negative attitudes can influence behavior in terms of relating to people from different cultures. But if I say to the person who engages in this bad behavior that he must also love the individual that he hit, he would say that inside himself he can think whatever he wants. And he is right. But we are finding that over time when we institutionalize the norms of appropriate behaviors, people get used to the idea and begin to associate these improved behaviors with more positive attitudes. It's a slow process and it takes a great deal of time. The ultimate goal is to have people accept each other regardless of background and culture. Accepting them for whatever they are. It's a new field of study in Japan, but I think the Japanese people are learning, as we are.

In describing Jewish activities in the ghettoes, which Dr. Sandberg characterized as unarmed resistance, I noticed that he used the word "we"—"We organized schools. We educated our children." He might not have noticed himself. Perhaps it was because education, in the fullest sense of the word, has been his way of living in the post-Holocaust age as a Jew. Education of Jews. Education of other people in America and in Asia.

He also taught me that one has to be honest with himself to be able to learn and grow. I was profoundly touched by his honesty when he told me that he had been overjoyed at the news of dropping of the atomic bombs. He was twenty years old at that time and being trained to become a naval officer. After the training he was to be sent back to the Pacific for the invasion of Japan. Being killed in action was a realistic possibility. Then, the atomic bombs saved his life.

"All of us went crazy. We even threw the furniture....We really didn't think about the human suffering that the atomic bombs brought to the people in Hiroshima and Nagasaki. All we knew was that Germany and Japan were defeated, the war was over and we were saved." After telling me this story Dr. Sandberg added, "I think this is the first time I told a Japanese person about my reaction to the dropping of the atomic bombs. We were conditioned to believe that they were enemies and trained to dislike them and try to kill them." As I listened, I remembered him once telling me that his ship had been attacked by a Japanese submarine near the Aleutian island of Attu in 1944. And I could not help but be amazed at how far he had traveled from being a young seaman in that ship to the person who was now in front of me. I asked him which he thought was easier to teach people to hate or to love. Dr. Sandberg answered, "It is probably easier to teach hatred than to teach love, but it is much more satisfying to teach love."

NOTES

[1] Bruce M. Ramer and Neil C. Sandberg, "Books Untrue to Japan-Jewish History," *Japan Times*, Jan. 21, 1990.

Wallenberg Inspires Us To Be Better Human Beings

Annette Lantos
Wife of US Congressman Tom Lantos

"Whoever saves one life, saves the world entire." I learned that these words were from the Talmud. There is no better way to describe the actions of the Righteous Gentiles. Their courage not only saved the lives of the Jewish people but also our faith in humanity. Elie Wiesel, a Holocaust survivor and Nobel Peace Prize winning writer once said, "In those times, one climbed to the summit of humanity by simply remaining human."[1] Chiune Sugihara, a Japanese diplomat who issued thousands of visas to fleeing Jewish refugees and Oskar Schindler, a German industrialist who saved his Jewish workers were among those who remained human during the darkest moment of history. Their actions restore our beliefs that there is goodness, love, and compassion within ourselves.

And here is a man who not only remained human but also single-handedly confronted the evil to save innocent Jews. Although his story became a shining example of courage in the hearts of millions of people around the world, he himself had to spend his life after the war in a Russian prison cell.

I first learned about Raoul Wallenberg in 1981 when President Ronald Reagan declared this Swedish diplomat, who saved 100,000 Hungarian Jews during the final days of World War II, as an honorary U.S. citizen. I wondered who this man was receiving the coveted honor only Winston Churchill and few others were given. Since then, I tried to follow Wallenberg's story.

Unlike other Righteous Gentiles who happened to be there to

save the Jews, Raoul Wallenberg went out of his way to rescue the Jews in Budapest. After occupying Hungary in March of 1944, the Germans sent the Jews living in the countryside to Auschwitz at an astonishing rate of 12,000 a day.[2] The remaining 200,000 Jews in Budapest were about to face the same fate of Eichmann's "Final Solution." Wallenberg was to rescue as many Jews as possible by negotiations, threats, and even bribes. He was given the blessing for this mission by the United States government who finally decided to help the remnants of European Jews from the Nazi atrocity.

In January 1944, the United States, after years of a "win the war first" policy, created the War Refugee Board which would be in charge of implementing the policy of rescuing Jews. And the U.S. turned to neutral Sweden to look for a person who could go to Budapest to engage in a rescue operation.

Raoul Wallenberg was born in 1912 into a prominent banking family in Sweden, equivalent of Mitsui or Mitsubishi in Japan. His father died a few month before his birth. So, it was under the influence of his grandfather, Gustav Wallenberg who served as an ambassador to Japan in the early 1900s, that Raoul grew up. Going to the United States to study architecture at the University of Michigan was also senior Wallenberg's idea. But the challenge awaiting this determined young aristocrat, who was fluent in several languages and was a brilliant negotiator, was one that human history had never witnessed. Wallenberg took up on that challenge without hesitation.

He arrived in Budapest in July of 1944 and immediately started organizing the rescue effort. He issued thousands of Swedish protective passports, "Shutzpass," to Jews. Although its appearance was very official, this passport type document had no legal basis. It was Wallenberg's invention to buy time for the Jews in Budapest. He often personally intervened to rescue Jews who were about to be sent to Auschwitz in cattle cars. When Eichmann, upon learning that the railroad to the death camps had been bombed, ordered Jews to walk to the border, Wallenberg followed the death march to try to save as many Jews as possible.

He bought many houses in Budapest which he declared as Swedish Safe Houses where the Jews could be under the Swedish protection. Considering that Wallenberg was only 31 years old when he arrived in Budapest, it was amazing that, in a very short period of time, he could establish hospitals, soup kitchens, and other necessary systems by using hundreds of Jewish volunteers.

Wallenberg even arranged a face-to-face meeting with Adolph Eichmann, who would be tried and hanged 16 years later in Israel, and criticized the Nazi philosophy. This principal architect of the "Final Solution" was said to have left with a warning, "Accidents do happen, even to a neutral diplomat."[3] Indeed, by the end of 1944 Wallenberg had to sleep in a different place each night because he was being hunted by the Arrow Cross, the Hungarian Nazis. When advised by a colleague to stop the rescue efforts and to take shelter with neutral diplomats, he refused by saying, "I have taken upon myself this mission and I would never be able to return to Stockholm without knowing that I've done everything that stands in a man's power to rescue as many Jews as possible."[4]

Wallenberg was unique in that he refused to see Jews as anything but fellow human beings when the perpetrators, bystanders, and even victims themselves ceased to do so. One woman who was rescued from the death march by Wallenberg later said,

> Our spirit was broken. We felt like animals...people didn't even talk to each other. Everyone was overwhelmed by his own personal horror.... Suddenly, at one corner, we saw some people coming in with civilian clothes, with flashlights and a megaphone. And that was Wallenberg.... He told us that he had demanded that those who possessed Shutzpasses should be allowed to return to Budapest...Can you understand what his presence meant to this condemned group? Somebody who had no obligation to us—he fought for us—he saw us as human beings—worth saving! It was a magical presence. It changed our mood.... He gave us back our humanness.[5]

Wallenberg's most spectacular victory in rescuing the Jews came only a few days before the Russian troops finally arrived in Budapest. Not forgetting Eichmann's order for total annihilation, Germans and the Arrow Cross were gathering for the final assault on the city's central ghetto with nearly 63,000 Jews inside. Upon learning about the imminent attack, he wrote a note to the German general who was in charge of defending Budapest. His message was, "If this pogrom proceeds and Jews die, I will personally testify at the War Crimes Tribunal and see that you are hanged for murder."[6] The German general ordered cancellation of the assault at the last minute and the entire Jewish population of the ghetto was saved.

Wallenberg's mission was to be accomplished when the Russian troops arrived in the city. But he was already thinking about restoring the lives of Budapest's citizens. He wrote in his plan:

> For many months now I have witnessed the suffering of the Hungarian people and, if it is not too presumptuous to say so, I think I have participated in it spiritually to such an extent that it has now become my suffering. Because of my involvement, I have been able to recognize the great need for speedy humanitarian relief and reconstruction activities.[7]

So, it was to ask for food for the Jews that Wallenberg went to see the Red Army commander who had set up his headquarters outside Budapest. It turned out that the day Wallenberg left to meet the Russians, January 17, 1945, was the last day the world saw him as a free man.

The Russian government first denied that Wallenberg was in their country. Then in 1957, after 12 years since his disappearance, it acknowledged that Wallenberg had been imprisoned at Lubyanka prison in Moscow and had died there in 1947 as a result of a heart attack.[8] Yet, rumors that the Swedish diplomat was alive in the Russian Gulag persisted as reports of Wallenberg being sighted continued to reach to the West throughout the 60s and 70s. Wallenberg's mother spent her entire life after the war trying to get her son back from the Russian prison. She asked the often reluctant Swedish government to keep inquiring of the Soviet Union about her son's fate. She also sought the expertise of the famous Nazi-hunter, Simon Wiesenthal, telling him, "If you could find Eichmann, surely you can find my son."[9] The Simon Wiesenthal Center, a Jewish human rights organization, in Los Angeles ran an ad in New York Times on December 7, 1987, when then Soviet President Mikhail Gorbachev visited the United States. It read, "An American hero has been missing since 1945. One word from Mr. Gorbachev could find him." In 1991, however, the Soviet government reiterated its previous statement that Wallenberg had died in 1947.[10]

The story I found about Raoul Wallenberg was, therefore, a profoundly sad one. Knowing him as a young man before he spent the fateful six months in Budapest was even more painful for I could see how he had been full of life and how eagerly he had been looking to the future. His optimism, curiosity, a remarkable insight into human nature, and willingness to face a challenge were all to be utilized later when he engaged in rescuing Jews in Budapest. Looking at his pictures in those blissful days made it particularly difficult for me to imagine him being alone somewhere in the Russian Gulag.

Then I became interested in those who were saved by Wallenberg. How have they felt all these years knowing that while they could enjoy peace and freedom, the person who made it all possible for them was in the prison? The United States Congressman Tom Lantos (D-California) and his wife Annette were both saved by Wallenberg when they were teenagers in Budapest. Congressman Lantos wrote a very eloquent tribute to Wallenberg as foreword to *Wallenberg: Lost Hero.*

> Wallenberg went out of his way, leaving behind the comfort and affluence, the safety and security of Stockholm to go to Budapest—and I know what Budapest was like in those last hellishly ugly months of World War II. Wallenberg put his life on the line day in and day out for people he did not know because he believed in the right of every human being to live.
>
> Neither I, nor my wife, nor our children nor our grandchildren would be here today if it were not for Raoul Wallenberg. During that whole dark nightmare, no one else directly confronted Nazi cruelty. No one else had the audacity to follow the death marches, to jump in front of guns leveled at Jews, to pull people off deportation trains. Raoul Wallenberg not only saved 100.000 lives, he saved our faith in humanity.
>
> In history, one can find many men who have killed 100,000 people. But how many have saved 100,000? Wallenberg has shown us that one individual—motivated by a genuine and personal concern for human rights—can face evil and triumph; that one person alone can make a difference; that there are genuine heroes to illuminate our age."[11]

He added that his wife "more than anyone else was responsible for bringing international attention to Raoul Wallenberg."[12] So I wrote them a letter asking for an interview. Mrs. Lantos immediately responded letting me know that she would be happy to meet with me.

Congressman Lantos, the only survivor of the Holocaust in the United States Congress, is the founder and co-chairman of the 200-member bipartisan Congressional Human Rights Caucus, the umbrella human rights organization of Congress. He is serving on the Government Reform and Oversight Committee and the International Relations Committee as well as representing the U.S. Congressional Delegation to the European Parliament.

When I visited his district office in San Francisco Mrs. Lantos greeted me by saying, "Your letter was so special that I looked forward to seeing you." In her small office she started to talk about her experience.

> When the Nazi occupied Hungary in March, 1944, our family could seek shelter in the Portuguese Embassy since my father was a rather prominent businessman in Budapest. I was 13 years old at that time. Tom, who was 16, was made to work in a forced labor camp. We met each other when we were 6 and 10 and knew from the very beginning that we would marry someday.
>
> As we would later learn, Raoul Wallenberg arrived in Budapest in July of 1944. He immediately negotiated with the Germans that they recognize the Swedish passports he was issuing by the hundreds to Jews. Wallenberg was a brilliant negotiator. He threatened, cajoled, and bribed. And because of the agreement that Wallenberg negotiated, other neutral nations' passports also became valid. That was how my mother and I got out of Hungary with Portuguese passports in October of 1944. My father could not come with us and later was killed. Tom also lost his parents but was saved by living under one of the Swedish houses that Wallenberg had set up. Wallenberg was so bold that he dressed young Jews, like Tom, who were blond and blue-eyed in a SS uniform to let them go outside to get food or medicine.
>
> After the war we came to the United States and got married. We did not talk about the Holocaust because the only way we could handle the horrible things that had happened to us was by forgetting them.

Then in 1958, two years after the aborted Hungarian uprising against Russia, I received a package from my aunt in Budapest. At that time Hungary was totally closed behind the iron curtain. I couldn't understand how the package could ever get through because it was unheard of to get any communication from Hungary in those days.

When I opened it I found this incredible Hagadah, which is a prayer book that Jewish people use only during the Passover Holiday. Inside the Hagadah, there was a beautiful letter written to me by my father on April 6, 1939. A totally prophetic letter! He foresaw exactly what was going to happen to us. He also foresaw that he was not going to survive the coming storm. Indeed he was killed, shot and thrown into the Danube, in January of 1945. He foresaw in 1939 that we were going to lose the wonderful life we had, that everything would be destroyed. And he foresaw that as a result of all the tragedy, I was going to lose my faith in God. He also realized that he was not going to be my side to try to revive my faith. So, he wrote me this beautiful letter asking me that no matter how much tragedy there would be in our lives, I must not lose my faith in God because that faith in God would ultimately be justified.

I received this letter 14 years after my father was killed in the Holocaust. All the nice things we had possessed before the war were destroyed or taken away from us. How did this book survive, how did my aunt get hold of it, and how did she get permission to send it to me? It was unbelievable that I was, in 1958, holding this book with the letter from my father written to me in 1939, before he died, before all these things had begun to happen. It really changed my whole life.

Up to that point I had lost all connection with my roots, with my faith and with God. And like so many other Jewish people, we never told our children that we were Jews. My two daughters had no idea about our background except that we were from Hungary. My father's letter changed all that. I wanted to make some sense, some meaning, something of value in this dark hole of history in which I was forced to go.

It was the same for Tom. When the Germans occupied Hungary all the young people were taken to the forced labor camp. He was forced to dig air raid shelters because by then carpet bombings were coming from both the West and East. But the Jewish workers were not allowed to go into the shelter while the military used them for their protection. So, when the air raid came, Tom was lying on the ground writing a letter to me. I still have all those letters. I will never forget one letter in which he wrote, "Everybody around me is dead. I am the only survivor of this air raid. I must believe now that maybe God has saved me for a purpose."

Since then we began to talk about the Holocaust with our daughters. We did not want to tell them about it solely in terms of Jewish helplessness or the human capacity of senseless cruelty, but rather, in a way that would give them an appreciation of man's capacity for heroism in the face of despair. For us, Wallenberg seemed a clear example. I began talking to high school students about Wallenberg and it became my career.

At that time we thought Wallenberg had died in 1947. Then on November 7, 1977, Tom read a brief paragraph in the *New York Times* in which the famous Nazi-hunter Simon Wiesenthal was quoted as saying that he had located Wallenberg alive in a Soviet mental hospital. Imagine our surprise! Tom and I wanted to rescue Wallenberg from the Soviet prison. We placed ads in various Jewish papers and urged readers to write to the White House, their congressmen, the Secretary of State, and even the Soviet government.

Then a miracle happened. While I was driving my car in the fall of 1979, National Public Radio was announcing that President Carter would conduct a public call-in program on the air. When I heard the PO Box number that we should send our request to speak with the president I could not write it down so I kept repeating the number until I got home. I ran into my house and wrote the number down and sent ten postcards. We were instructed not to write the question because Carter wanted the questions to be random and spontaneous.

Two weeks later, as I was leaving the house to pick up my mother at the airport the telephone rang. I was told that my postcard was one of the ten that had been selected at random from over 24,000. In a moment President Carter would be on the line to answer my question on national radio. And in a moment my life was changed.

Mrs. Lantos showed me a newspaper article that carried her conversation with President Carter. She told me that only ten minutes after she finished talking to the president a reporter appeared at the door of her house.

> *Lantos:* Mr. President when my husband and I were youngsters in Hungary during World War II, our lives were saved through the intervention of a Swedish diplomat named Raoul Wallenberg. We later learned that Mr. Wallenberg who also saved the lives of thousands of other Jewish people like us, was acting on behalf of the American State Department. But unfortunately Mr. Wallenberg was arrested at the end of the war by the Russians and has been in Russia ever since. Although the Russians claim that he died, there is an overwhelming amount of evidence which indicates that he is still alive in a Soviet prison. Could you do something, Mr. President, to get him released?

> *Carter:* There's a limit to what I can do. We have inquired into the Wallenberg case with the Russians both when I was in Vienna this year with President Brezhnev and other Russian leaders and through the Soviet ambassador here in Washington and also our ambassador in Moscow. On occasion, when Secretary Vance has met with Foreign Minister Gromyko, we've also inquired about the Wallenberg case along with the cases of many others. The Soviets maintain their claim that Mr. Wallenberg is no longer alive, but we are not forgetting about this case and will continue our efforts.

> *Lantos:* Thank you very much, Mr. President I hope you will.[13]

From that day—October 13, 1979—the world suddenly became interested in Raoul Wallenberg. Television, newspaper, and magazine reporters were eager to know about Wallenberg. I spent weeks talking to them. At that time, Tom was a college professor. The next year, he ran for the U.S. Congress and was elected.

The very first piece of legislation that Tom introduced in the Congress was a resolution that would make Wallenberg an honorary U.S. citizen. At the beginning we were told that there was no chance that this would be passed. But, the day before this bill came to the Judiciary Committee, the chairman of the committee just happened to turn on his TV and saw a program about Wallenberg I had been on. That was totally accidental. The next morning I was sitting in the front row of the committee hearing. The chairman called me up to him and said, "Now I know the Wallenberg story. I am going to mark up your legislation." Later the House passed it unanimously and on October 5, 1981 President Reagan signed the resolution.

By this legislation, Wallenberg became an honorary citizen of the United States. His welfare was now officially a concern of our government. At that time I still believed that Wallenberg was alive. So, just as Wallenberg had saved tens of thousands of Hungarian Jews by declaring them to be under Swedish protection, we were giving the United States a legitimate reason to press the Soviet leaders for his release.

And then a few weeks later, I had an incredible feeling. I woke up in the middle of the night crying. I knew that he was dead. Up until then, every year we heard about him, from some witnesses who came out. But from that time on, after that day in 1981, not a word. I knew that night, he died. He did not die in 1947 or during 60s and 70s, but I believe he died in 1981.

So, this is my story. Whatever Wallenberg's fate in Soviet prisons may be, in the deepest and most profound sense, Wallenberg lives. We honor him, we remember him, and his story inspires us to be better human beings and more valiant in our struggle to build a better and safer world.'

Mrs. Lantos talked to me for almost three hours. We shared emotional moments together when she talked about the letter her father had written to her, or about her mother's courage in letting 13- year-old Mrs. Lantos cross the border to Switzerland alone in the night so she might live. "Those were tough times," she said. "But, we are a big family now. We have 17 grandchildren!" When I was about to leave she embraced me and said, "When I started all this I was about your age, so keep doing what you believe is important."

On my flight back to Los Angeles, I remembered the profound sadness I had felt when I had first learned about Wallenberg. For 15 years I have been asking myself, "What should one do upon learning such an overwhelming story that touches each individual in a most personal way?" Mrs. Lantos said, "Wallenberg inspires us to be better human beings." Have I finally found an answer?

NOTES

[1] Michael Berenbaum, *The World Must Know* (New York: Little Brown and Company, 1993), 157.

[2] Katy Marton, *Wallenberg: Missing Hero* (New York: Arcade Publishing, 1995), 38.

[3] Danny Smith, *Wallenberg: Lost Hero* (Springfield, Ill: Templegate Publishers, 1987), 107.

[4] *Ibid.*, 12.

[5] Abraham Cooper, "Wallenberg Held Hostage: Day 14,000," *Jewish Chicago*, July, 1982, 36.

[6] Smith, *Wallenberg: Lost Hero*, 115.

[7] Smith, *Wallenberg: Lost Hero*, 118-19.

[8] *Ibid.*, 190-91.

[9] Hella Pick, *Simon Wiesenthal* (Boston: Northeastern Press, 1996), 236-38.

[10] Marton, *Wallenberg: Missing Hero*, 219-20.

[11] Smith, *Wallenberg: Lost Hero*, 7-8.

[12] *Ibid.*, 6.

[13] Annette Lantos, "My Fight for Raoul Wallenberg," *Moment*, October, 1987, 24.

The Mission Sugihara Would Be Proud of

Leo Melamed
Chairman Emeritus and Senior Policy Advisor
Chicago Mercantile Exchange

"Leo Melamed is a legend," so I was told. He is chairman emeritus of the Chicago Mercantile Exchange and considered "the father of financial futures," of which I knew nothing except it was conceived by him with the blessing of Nobel Prize winning economist Milton Friedman.

In the early summer of 1991, I was working on a research project on women in the U.S. futures industry, a job offered to me by a Japanese futures industry magazine. I needed money to cover my tuition for law school the following fall. After reading a few books about the futures industry, I boldly started interviews with some of the most prominent women in the industry, including Wendy Gramm who was chairwoman of the Commodity Futures Trading Commission (CFTC), the government regulatory agency with oversight of futures markets, and wife of Texas senator Phil Gramm.

As I interviewed more women, I began to feel the presence of one person behind all these women all of whom talked about the equal opportunity they enjoyed in their careers. That person was Leo Melamed, who, as chairman of the Chicago Mercantile Exchange for more than two decades, spearheaded promoting equality for women and minorities in the futures industry. So, it was a logical step for me to interview him. As it turned out, my encounter with Mr. Melamed provided me with more than a finishing touch for the project.

Black twin tower buildings of the Chicago Mercantile Exchange
stand along the Chicago River just a few blocks north of the Sears
Tower, the world's tallest building. I was to meet Mr. Melamed there
in June of 1991. Upon entering his room, the first thing I noticed
was a large poster by Ben Shahn, a Jewish artist, displayed on the
wall. It said, "You have not converted a man because you have si-
lenced him." From the very beginning, I realized that this person
was extraordinary, not only as a business leader but also as a human
being. One reporter described him:

> Dark, diminutive, with a receding hairline that emphasized his
> piercing brown eyes, Melamed was not an overpowering physical
> presence on the trading floor. But his voice, his facility with words,
> and his ability to sense the will of a crowd made Melamed an
> overnight political force at the Merc (Chicago Mercantile Ex-
> change). Over the years, his clear tenor and carefully cadenced
> phrasing would become a siren song that would help transform
> the Merc from a fading butter-and-egg exchange to the second
> largest commodities exchange in the world. "I'm a leader. That's
> my makeup," he once told an interviewer. "I don't know how to
> do anything except lead."[1]

The person I met on that day, however, was not a legend nor was he
the awesome figure I had expected. I found Leo Melamed to be a
person of unwavering commitment to what he believed in, including equality for women and minorities, as well as warm and person-
able. "Many reporters come here to interview me, but I believe you
are the first one asking about my philosophy regarding equal rights
for women in the futures industry," he told me. For almost an hour
he talked about his role in dropping female prohibitions on the trading floor and in introducing the very first woman trader in the previ-
ously all-male pits.

Although I was deeply impressed by his long-held beliefs, it was
a meeting with another person, who personified his beliefs, that really made me see Mr. Melamed's true humanity. After the interview,
he suggested that I meet Ms. Valerie Turner, the Chief Operating
Officer of his firm and an African American lady. She started working for Mr. Melamed in 1959 as a secretary when she was 18. But as

he became more involved in the Merc, she gradually assumed the responsibility of running his firm with his complete trust. And this was long before women's liberation or affirmative action changed the landscape of the American workforce. To him, her gender or the color of her skin did not matter. All he saw was her ability. I was truly amazed when she told me, "Mr. Melamed and I have been very good partners." It was obvious from her poise that not only did he give her a chance but also treated her with respect, a relationship which I had a hard time imagining in a Japanese corporate culture.

After that day, I did not expect to see him again. I would finish the project and turn it in to the magazine, probably never thinking about the futures industry again. Then, while I was doing further research on him, I came across incredible sentences in a book which had just come out. It read, "...Melamed fled Poland eastward in 1939, as the clouds of World War II gathered over Europe. He was six years old then, and nearly nine by the time a freighter from Tokyo brought his family to America."[2]

I could not help but wonder if he had been saved by Chiune Sugihara, a Japanese consul general in Lithuania in the summer of 1940. How else could he escape from Poland, land in Japan, and finally sail to the U.S. in those days? A friend of mine in New York, who was married to a Jewish American, had just visited the widow of Sugihara in Japan and had written an article for a newspaper in Scarsdale, NY. Her interview article with Mrs. Sugihara described her husband's courageous act of issuing thousands of transit visas to fleeing Jewish refugees a half century ago. I decided to send him a copy of the article together with my letter asking if he knew about this event.

That letter was a beginning of the correspondence between Mr. Melamed and me, which eventually led me to a decision to write a book on the Holocaust.

August 6, 1991
Dear Ms. Tokudome,

Thank you very much for your continued interest with respect to my immigration to the United States. I do believe that the late

Mr. Sugihara was indeed the Japanese consul in Kovno who provided my father with a transit visa to Japan which ultimately saved our lives. The story that you provided is, therefore, of great moment to me. I plan to transmit it to my children so they, too, can learn about these events.

I would also be happy to contact Mrs. Sugihara and personally thank her for her husband's heroic efforts on our behalf. Perhaps you could help me with such arrangements.

Sincerely,
Leo Melamed

August 9, 1991
Dear Mr. Melamed:

Thank you very much for your letter. I am very happy to know that I could be of help in your finding out the situation in which you immigrated to the United States.

Mrs. Sugihara's current address is as follows. I believe that she understands English. If you would like to have your letter translated into Japanese, however, I will be happy to do the translation.

Sincerely,
Kinue Tokudome

August 20, 1991
Dear Mrs. Sugihara:

I was a small child on September 1, 1939, when World War II broke out and the Germans captured my birthplace of Bialystok, Poland. In 1940 my father, mother and I found ourselves in Wilno, Lithuania, refugees, running first from the Nazis and later from the Russians. As you know, Wilno was later taken over by the Russians and my father, a well-known "anti-communist" was on the run again.

You can imagine my astonishment and surprise when I read

the article by Mrs. Kuniko Katz describing the courageous acts of your late husband, Mr. Senpo Sugihara, when he was Japanese Consul in Kovno, Lithuania in 1940. Indeed, the transit visas he issued to Jewish refugees saved their lives for it gave them the required "credentials" with which to request permission to leave Russia.

I know the foregoing first-hand. My father, Isaac Melamdovich, received a transit visa to Japan from your husband in 1940 which resulted in saving our three lives. The remainder of our family was at some point ushered into the synagogue of Bialystok together with all the Jews that could be crammed within, and burned to death.

We arrived in Japan in January of 1941 and spent some four months living under the serene skies of Kobe. I have the fondest memories of those days and have never forgotten the profound truth that Japan saved our lives. In April of 1941, we arrived in the United States.

It gives me the greatest pleasure to write this letter and extend my deepest respect and gratitude to the memory of your late husband. He was a humanitarian in the fullest sense of the word and should be remembered as one of the heroes of World War II.

Very truly yours,
Leo Melamed

cc: Mrs. Kuniko Katz
        Mrs. Kinue Tokudome

January 12, 1994
Dear Mr. Melamed,

Seeing "Schindler's List" brought back the wonderful memory of you and Mr. Sugihara. If you have seen the movie already, I am sure you are thinking about the event in Lithuania in 1940.

I am planning to write an article about what happened to those who were saved by Mr. Sugihara for a Japanese newspaper. I would appreciate your comments on "Schindler's List" or on the lessons that we have or have not learned from the history. I would like Japanese readers to know that the Holocaust is not something that happened a long time ago in a far away place that has nothing to do with the present day Japanese people but an event whose legacy still lives on today.

Sincerely,
Kinue Tokudome

January 26, 1994
Dear Kinue,

I was happy to hear from you again as I have such fond memories of our conversation together. I am also grateful for the favorable articles which you wrote about me.

I certainly am willing to assist you in anyway I can along the lines you suggest. In the next few days, I will provide you with some paragraphs about my feelings after seeing "Schindler's List" as well as the lessons that all of this has taught the world.

Best wishes.
Leo Melamed

February 7, 1994
Dear Kinue,

As promised in my response to your recent letter, the following are some of my thoughts with respect to Ambassador Sugihara and "Schindler's List:"

It is nearly impossible to put to words my feelings upon seeing "Schindler's List." The movie represented an emotional watershed for me since only by the grace of God did my parents and I escape the fate that awaited so many millions of my ethnic nation—a fate so vividly depicted in this film. Words are inadequate to explain the depth of my pain and anger.

Perhaps the overriding emotion that Schindler's List evoked in me was the unanswerable question: Where was the rest of the world?

How could so satanic an event occur in the twentieth

century of human experience? How could this barbaric event take place with the rest of civilization blindly closing their eyes? Where were the political leaders of the civilized world during the years of the Holocaust? Where were the leaders of the world's great religions? Where were the cultural leaders of society? Where were the voices of social consciousness? Where were the writers, poets, the philosophers? Where were the decent ordinary people in the world?

I have found no satisfactory answers to these questions.

The only glimmer of hope that is offered in response to these questions are the brave deeds of a precious few who like Raoul Wallenberg and Oskar Schindler stood up to the insanity around them. The actions of Ambassador Sugihara in 1940 place him also within this select group of human beings. We owe these representatives of our civilization an incalculable debt: Their actions preserved a small portion of human dignity.

The project you undertake in writing is commendable. Keep up the good work. If I can be of further assistance, please contact me.

Sincerely,
Leo Melamed

March 20, 1994
Dear Mr. Melamed,

I am sending you a copy of the article which I wrote about you for Yomiuri America, a Japanese newspaper, with the English translation. I quoted most of what you had written for me. I hope you will find the article to be satisfactory.

I feel fortunate that I was touched by this story in a personal way. Thank you very much for sharing your thoughts with me.

Sincerely,
Kinue Tokudome

January 30, 1995
Dear Mr. Melamed,

On January 15th, I had the most moving experience I would
never forget. More than 1,500 people gave a standing ovation to
Mrs. Sugihara who was honored at the dinner commemorating
the 50th anniversary of the liberation of the concentration camps.
The dinner was organized by the Simon Wiesenthal Center here
in Los Angeles and attended by many prominent people including Steven Spielberg and Ann Richards.

I was able to talk to Mrs. Sugihara and her eldest son who told
me that you had visited them last year. Attending the dinner
made me feel that I too, would like to do things, however small
it may be, to promote a better understanding between Jewish
people and Japanese people.

Sincerely,
Kinue Tokudome

November 29, 1996
Dear Mr. Melamed,

I was delighted to find your name in the acknowledgment sec-
tion of Professor Hillel Levine's recent book, *In Search of Sugihara*.
I think that the book is a very moving account of the author's
personal journey to find out who Mr. Sugihara really was, and
that he did a very honest job writing about his findings.

As for myself, I, too, am working on a book project right now.
It will introduce to the Japanese readers those people who try to
make the world remember the Holocaust and the lessons it has
taught. Ever since I first met you, this topic somehow never left
me.

I would appreciate it if you let me interview you for this book.

I very much look forward to hearing from you soon.

Sincerely yours,
Kinue Tokudome

So, it was on January 28, 1997, that I visited Mr. Melamed again in Chicago, the city I had left five years earlier. His firm was now called Sakura Dellsher, Inc., a global futures organization he had formed with the Sakura Bank in 1993.

You haven't changed since I first met you six years ago.

It's been six years!

Yes, almost. Today, I would like to hear about your experience of escaping from the Nazis and being saved by Mr. Sugihara. What do you remember about those days?

Oh, I remember a great deal, probably because I was at such an impressionistic age. I was but a small child living in a small Polish city when suddenly the war broke out. I was taken out of school, running across borders, hiding with my parents in places in Wilno, running to Moscow, taken on the trans-Siberian railway, and then on a Japanese boat. I was eight years old when we landed in Japan. All of those things left an enormous impression on me. These were highly unusual events for an eight-year-old. I never forgot them; they are carved into memory for the rest of my life. I remember one winter night in early January 1941, when we arrived in Vladivostok, we had to wait while our baggage was searched by the Russians. Then finally, at one in the morning, we were brought on board a Japanese junk boat, a little boat I would learn the next day. The Siberian wind was blowing, maybe it was 20 degrees below zero outside. This scene could only be pictured in a movie, people being transferred onto a boat with all their belongings and then laying down on the floor, and then waking in the morning to a boat that was rocking, a tiny little Japanese junk boat. People were sick all around me. I never got seasick. I don't even get seasick to this day. After three days on this Japanese boat we arrived at Tsuruga. The difference between the Siberian cold and Tsuruga was like night and day. Here was a beautiful sky, mountains all around, and people were wearing colorful kimonos.

Do you remember how your parents were upon reaching Japan?

I do remember because I was very sensitive to the feelings and fears that my parents had exhibited throughout the trip. My father was hunted by the Russians because he was a very outspoken writer against communism. So, it was first running away from the Nazis and then from the Bolsheviks. It was a very difficult period, and my parents always exhibited this enormous fear. There was the unquestionable realization transmitted to me that this was a dangerous time. When we got to Japan, all that changed. No real fear, no one was chasing us. It was as if someone suddenly lifted the curtain and a new world came upon us.

What do you remember most in Japan?

Everything in Japan was colorful and people were friendly. I particularly remember one Japanese gentleman who helped us when we were going to go visit our refugee friend in Kobe but got lost. This gentleman, who was on his way to work, spent the next hour helping us find the address. He would not let us go until he was sure that we had found the place we were going. And the impression that it left on us, we all talked about afterwards, was "What courteous people!" He knew we were lost and went out of his way to help us. Well, I have to tell you that was never forgotten by any one of us. For years and years, my mother would talk about the gentleness, courteousness and friendliness of all the people in Japan. And these were the people who didn't even know us and most of them had never seen Westerners. Yet there was this feeling of friendship.

Do you find the same quality in Japanese people today? Of course, we are materially a much richer nation now, and we know much more about the world.

I would say yes. I still see the same decency, the same friendliness and the same outgoingness to the foreigners. But I will tell you where I had the biggest problem. When the war broke out between Japan and the United States in 1941, the propaganda, of course, was very anti-Japanese. They were the enemy and we were at war. And I had difficulty with that because I remembered that

Japanese were such a nice people. Now I was nine or ten years old, and I saw a movie where Japanese people were pictured as a bad people. I couldn't understand them. These weren't the people that I knew. But these movies only showed Japanese soldiers. So, pretty soon I got an impression in my mind as a child, "Well, soldiers are different from regular people."

How did all these experiences shape your views on human beings?

I think we are all a product of our parents. My parents were great humanitarians. They believed in the equality of all people. My mother was perhaps one of the early pioneers of the women's movement. But, it was the Sugihara experience that had the greatest impact on me. My father had told me that it was a great humanitarian act performed by Sugihara—for which he received no money, no prestige, and no visible value. He also told me that Sugihara knew that we were all Jews and that it didn't matter to him, which was another enormous lesson. After all why did Sugihara do it? Here was a Japanese person without any prejudice at all. All he saw was that he could save those Jews just by signing his name, and he did it. That's not something you ever forget, certainly not me, because I wouldn't be here but for Sugihara's humanitarian act.

Are you presently involved in any activity relating to the Holocaust?

Absolutely. I am extremely involved. I was appointed first by President Bush and then again by President Clinton as a member of the U.S. Holocaust Memorial Museum in Washington, D.C. I recently took a hand, together with other Council members, on the creation of the Committee on Conscience. It is a little more than three years of my work. The idea of the Committee on Conscience will be that if there is an attempt of genocide ever again, like the one in Bosnia, we will speak up and make a very loud noise using the moral and powerful voice of the Holocaust Memorial Museum. That committee is now launched, I am very proud of my efforts to make that happen. And I hope that is a contribution Mr. Sugihara would be proud of.

In the course of our conversation I found out that Mr. Melamed had written a book, *Leo Melamed: Escape to the Futures*, in the previous year. I apologized to him for not having known about the book and promised to read it. So, I spent a few days after I came back from Chicago reading his book. It was his personal account of his escape from the Nazis as a child that eventually led him to the futures market where he became the most influential figure himself. As *The New York Times Book Review* said, "Few memoirs begin as memorably as Leo Melamed's,"[3] the book began with his escape, with his parents, from the Nazis and later the Russians. I was startled to find out that his father had received his life-saving visa on the very day Sugihara was leaving Lithuania, August 31, 1940.[4]

It was also a beautiful tribute to his truly remarkable parents, to whom he dedicated the book. In every sentence he described his parents, both of whom had now passed away, I saw his deep love, respect and affection for them. They were Bundists, who believed in a secular and modern Jewish culture based on Yiddish as the language of the masses.[5] In poignant sentences, he remembered the night when his parents took 10-year-old Mr. Melamed to listen to Shloyme Mendelson, one of the world's leading literary figures in Yiddish and famous Bundist, whose words left a lasting impression on him: "The only way to achieve immortality is to connect your life to something that transcends mortality. And that something is an ideal."[6] For Mr. Melamed, his father was a person who had an ideal, who was devoting his life to doing something for the world, for the community and for Jews and for Yiddish.[7] He wrote that he joined the U.S. Holocaust Memorial Council when a famous Holocaust survivor and friend of his late father, Benjamin Meed, told him, "To honor your father's memory, you ought to get involved with the Museum.... As a survivor, you owe this debt."[8]

Creating a Committee on Conscience was one of the original recommendations made in 1979 by the U.S. Holocaust Memorial Commission created under President Carter and headed by Elie Wiesel. It would consist of "distinguished moral leaders in America," who would call governmental and public attention to ongoing instances of genocide.[9] Because of political infighting, it had never been created[10] until Mr. Melamed reintroduced the concept. The mission which he hoped that Mr. Sugihara would be proud of was accomplished on June 14, 1995, when the Committee on Conscience became a permanent instrument of the United States Holocaust Museum. The Museum's powerful voice will be used to "alert the national conscience, influence policy makers, and stimulate worldwide action to confront and work to halt acts of genocide or crimes against humanity."[11]

After I finished reading his book, I wrote him a letter as I always did.

February 3, 1997
Dear Mr. Melamed,

I was delighted to see you again. I have to apologize that I did not know that you had published a book, which I have just finished reading. Having read your book I am totally convinced that it was my fate that I met you six years ago.

Before I met you, I had been a foreign student with two toddlers studying American politics at the University of Illinois Circle Campus and later a graduate student at the University of Chicago. By the time my children had entered grade school, my fascination with American politics and its underlying philosophy had led me to law school.

I am telling you all this because I now realize that everything happened for a reason. When I was standing outside the Union Station in Chicago in freezing temperature waiting for a bus to the Circle Campus, I did not fully understand why I was doing that. When I was struggling to keep up with much younger students at the University of Chicago while I had to commute from the suburb everyday after dropping my children at preschool, I did not fully understand why I was doing that. And when I sat in the very first class at Chicago Kent Law School, totally intimidated, I did not really know why I was there.

I now realize that all of those educational opportunities had prepared me for the book project I am working on now.

When I first met you I did not know much about your background, but when you started talking about your commitment to equal rights for women and minorities, I immediately knew that you were speaking with deep conviction. Now that I have read your book, I have a feeling that all the pieces of the puzzle fit into their places. Although I really wish I had been able to meet your parents, I saw them, in a way, through you at that time. That is why you left such a strong impression on me. And I am eternally grateful to you for providing a topic that is very important and that I can devote myself to.

I hope our paths will cross again someday. In the mean time, I wish your endeavors in business and in serving the United States Holocaust Memorial Council a continuing success.

Sincerely yours,
Kinue Tokudome

February 4, 1997
Dear Kinue,

I have been a devotee of letter writing my whole life and pride myself as an able letter writer. Thus, I can say with a degree of professional certainty that your letter of February 3, 1997 to me, was written in a most professional and intellectual manner and evidenced a great deal of "soul." Thank you for it.

Sincerely,
Leo Melamed

I thought this chapter on Mr. Melamed would be a heartwarming and inspiring story since his was one of the very few episodes in the history of the Holocaust that is uplifting. It was only after I met Mr. Miles Lerman, chairman of the United States Holocaust Memorial Council, under whose leadership Mr. Melamed serves, that I realized what we should learn from his experience. Mr. Lerman told me, "Mr. Melamed is the proof of what can happen when a person has the ability and is given the opportunity in a country like America. He's also the proof of what we had lost when a million and a half children perished in the Holocaust because he could have very easily been one of these million and a half children. Take a look at how far this man has reached. Take a look at how much he has done for America."

Whenever I open *I Never Saw Another Butterfly*, a collection of drawings and poems of children from Terezin concentration camp, I am struck by the tender age of these soon-to-be- killed victims. One boy, who was born in 1932 and deported to Auschwitz in 1944, described the ghetto as "a square kilometer of earth cut off from the world that's free."

Mr. Melamed personifies what might have been and what could have been for these children.

In addition to his childhood memories, *Leo Melamed: Escape to the Futures* chronicled many fascinating events such as his midnight telephone conversation with Fed Chairman Alan Greenspan after Black Monday or his being recruited by the White House to defend Hillary Rodham Clinton's cattle trading. Its Japanese edition, *Escape to the Futures*, is now available from Tokiwa Sogo Service, Inc.

NOTES

[1]David Greising, Laurie Morse, *Brokers, Bagmen & Moles* (New York: John Wiley & Sons, Inc., 1991), 107.

[2]*Ibid*, 106.

[3]"Leo Melamed: Escape to the Futures," *The New York Times Book Review*, September 22, 1996.

[4]Leo Melamed and Bob Tamarkin, *Leo Melamed: Escape to the Futures* (New York: John Wiley & Sons, Inc., 1996), 35. Hillel Levine, *In Search of Sugihara* (New York: The Free Press, 1996), 253.

[5]*Ibid.*, 21.

[6]*Ibid*, 24.

[7]*Ibid*, 23.

[8]*Ibid*, 423.

[9]Edward T. Linenthal, *Preserving Memory: The Struggle to Create America's Holocaust Museum* (New York: Viking Penguin, 1995), 37-38.

[10]*Ibid*, 263.

[11]Leo Melamed and Bob Tamarkin, *Leo Melamed: Escape to the Futures*, 423.

Dear Mr. Sugihara...

Hillel Levine
Professor of Sociology and Religion
Boston University

Dear Mr.Sugihara:

Is it "Chiune" or "Sempo?" Should I address you as "Mr. Sugihara" or the proper Japanese "Sugihara-san"? Or perhaps you would prefer the "Sergei Pavelovich Sugihara" of the Russian culture that you so loved, a culture closer to my own background and the thousands of my people whom you saved? Would you be uncomfortable were we to honor you with the Talmudic title "Reb Sugihara," meaning beloved master? Inconsequential questions, I know, but it is easier to evade the real awkwardness of trying to conjure you up, bring you to life.

Had I known you in your lifetime, I might have gone with you to Kaunas. You would have taken me through your former consulate, pointed to where the long lines formed. You would have walked me through the door that you kept open, shown me the window from which you persisted in observing and where you gave out the visas. But those were pre-Gorbachev days; how wary the Soviets would have made us. It may have been too hard to convey the meaning of No. 30 Vaizgantas street to them, like Mount Sinai of our tradition, significant only for what transpired, not for its humble form.

But if not for a walk in Kaunas, then perhaps Kamakura, your last home on Tokyo Bay. How happy I would have been strolling with you along the beach, the setting sun to the right of us. Mr. Fuji to the left, or would it be the setting sun to the left and Mr. Fuji to the right? Whatever, how badly I now feel and how much

I ask your forgiveness; we share this earth for forty years and I never came to see you.

I am feeling desperate and have nowhere to turn other than to you, directly. I have done everything I could to prepare for this time, when I must try to describe the moment you began to issue visas without constraints. And now I am riddled with anxiety. It is the feeling that those of us who are Jewish have at Neila, the closing moments of our Day of Atonement, the brink of final assessment. We have tried to do everything right. And yet we are so distant from our goal.

Since that day, several years ago, when I first stood in front of your consulate in Kaunas and imagined you starting to grant those visas, I felt this was a mysterious instant that must somehow be understood. Your act was so full of humanity, and so lacking in caution. To me, it has come to hold such profound meaning, a beacon of decency at a time when compassion was quickly disappearing from the world.

Suddenly, Jews were being pushed to the outside of the Western civilization they helped create—and then blamed for being outsiders! They were demonized as destructive outsiders, greedy and lecherous, who sucked the very marrow out of society, giving nothing in return. But you, you invited those outsiders in. You saw Jews as mothers and fathers and children, as people who cherished memory and harbored hope, you wondered where they slept and how they kept warm.

You worried what would become of them. You worried! How rare this was in a world racked with hate.

I have traveled to the four corners of the earth in search of people who once knew you: friends, colleagues, your disciples and bosses, your sister and her family, your first wife, Klaudia, and your second wife, Yukiko, your sons, daughters-in-law, grandchildren. The image that emerges consistently was that you were a man of extraordinary kindness and warmth, a cosmopolitan with special gifts for language, a man who felt at ease with people from diverse backgrounds, yet was also so very Japanese. All heartening information. Yet none of it explains why you opened your door to Jews when so few others did.

Each time I discover a new document about you I live in dread. This is the secret of Sugihara, I think, here is the smoking gun, the hidden motive. Now I will be compelled to recognize that a solitary act, the Act that appeared so pure, so expressive of the best that we might discover in human nature, was initiated from

other sources and prompted by other considerations....
*So tell me, Mr. Sugihara, Chiune/Sempo, Reb Sergei—again I stall
with anxiety—tell me, what did you do and why did you do it?*[1]

On April 1, 1997, New England was hit by an unusual spring snow storm. That week, I was to meet Professor Hillel Levine, the author of *In Search of Sugihara*, in Los Angeles. He called me to let me know that the Boston airport had been closed and that all the flights had been canceled. I had almost given up on our meeting when I received a phone call from him and learned that he had somehow managed to arrive in Los Angeles.

Professor Levine and I met at a restaurant in the Riviera Country Club where he was staying. We talked about our searches—his being that of Sugihara and mine of the people who told lessons of the Holocaust.

"While I was searching for Mr. Sugihara, I did not know what kind of a person I would find in the end." "But you have found the 'love of life' he possessed as a true motive behind his decisions to issue visas to Jewish refugees." "Yes, I have. I have found that he did it not as an act of self-sacrifice, but as something you and I could do if we had the 'love of life.'" "Are you happy that you have found it?" "Very much so. because I would like to teach my own children that they don't have to make sacrifice when they try to do good in this world, and that all they need is this 'love of life.'"

Thousands of Jewish refugees were saved because Mr. Sugihara had the "love of life." He did not want to see so many lives wasted. More than a half century later, he brought us—a professor of Judaic Studies and a Japanese writer—together. Had it not been for Sugihara's love of life, we never would have met each other. Professor Levine said to me when we were about to part, "Jewish people and Japanese people can be good friends."

Later I received a letter from Professor Levine which reads:

> In recent years I had heard about Sugihara, particularly on the several occasions when I was invited to Japan to teach Jewish history. The story made an impression on me. But, my first instinct, I must confess, was not to set aside everything in my life

to try to understand an obscure Japanese official about whom no one seemed to know anything. As important as rescuers were, it seemed to me, as much as we must honor people like Wallenberg and Schindler and the good French Protestants of Le Chambon, these rescue efforts were only a footnote; the Holocaust is about the murder of millions and millions. We dare not forget that and look for any on the other hands, any silverlinings, any comfort to our despair.

But in 1993 I was invited to Lithuania to inaugurate the Center for Judaic Studies at the University of Vilna. The irony of the renewal of Judaic Studies in the great city of Vilna, now with hardly any Jews left, was overwhelming. I was paralyzed by depression and could barely deliver my lectures and be convivial with my hosts. In this stark and deeply personal confrontation with the Holocaust and its consequences, I suddenly remembered the story I had heard in Japan about this Japanese do-gooder. I asked my hosts to take me to Kovno merely to see the place where he stood and distributed his visas. I stood outside the window out of which he looked and the door which he opened rather than slammed shut on needy people. I could not move. I could not stop thinking that something of great importance happened in this place that had implications for the future of humanity and that I had to try to understand it. And that was the beginning of the search....

My search for Sugihara has been, indeed, a search. It is a search to which I extend an invitation and helping hand to my readers to join me. And as with all profound searches in which we engage, it has been a search for more than a specific historical character. In searching for the man and in his Act, but also in trying to establish the motives behind his courageous efforts to rescue thousands of human beings, in examining Sugihara's inner life which nurtured those motives, we search for and try so hard to discover important parts of our selves.

The story that was told to me by his wife and older son and that is now repeated by others presents Sugihara as a stick figure, an uncomplicated goody-goody, a Japanese version of Job who did the right thing and then agonized over his unfair treatment. I wanted to understand the man who stood at the window of his consulate in Kovno, Lithuania during the summer of 1940 with thousands of desperate Jews, outside, asking for his help. I had a sense of him as a man who had no reason to endanger himself and his family by helping them. Like most Japanese of his generation, what he knew about Jews was largely negative: to him they were Shylocks from reading The Merchant of Venice in high school. Serving in the Japanese Army he learned that Jews were the dangerous communists who were trying to conquer the world. Neither did he share any of the personality traits of Schindler, the compulsive and invenerate gambler for whom outwitting the Nazis was the biggest gamble.

Sugihara had no reason to care for what was going on outside nor to identify with those Jews in any way. Yet when he looked out the window of the Japanese Consulate, he saw men, women, and children who he knew were going to be killed. So many other diplomats across Europe at the time, including American diplomats, often refused even the little help which they were authorized to provide to Jewish refugees. They closed their hearts and doors to people who they knew were in mortal danger. In the National Archives in Washington, I found the records of the American Consulate in Kovno. Among our consular officials, it became almost a contest to throw more and more obstacles at the feet of Jews who were fleeing. At this very moment, Chiune Sugihara began to issue visas that may have helped as many as 10,000 Jews escape. Why? That's what my book and portrait of Sugihara is all about.

What I have discovered about Sugihara leads me to believe that he was a far more complex man and a far better person than what others have claimed about him. And from what he did there are important lessons to be learnt. Chiune Sugihara did not reveal himself in any simple way. Perhaps because of that complexity and because—as I quickly discovered—his role as a consul was merely a disguise to his real role as a spy for the pro-Nazi faction of the Japanese Army and Foreign Ministry, it was not easy to uncover his trail nor to discover his personality. I was determined, however, because I believed that Sugihara's Act represents something very special in the history of morality. I, as a historian and a social scientist, did not have the tools to understand this, I sincerely felt. But if I got some glimpse into what made Sugihara tick, I would derive insights into the mystery of goodness that elucidate more than the history of this particular rescue effort.

The search was for Sugihara. I quickly discovered that Sugihara comes from the same background and the same training as some

Japanese officials who brought us the Rape of Nanjing, who perpetrated atrocities in China in the 1930s and against prisoners of war and in conquered territories during World War II. We have our stereotypes of Japanese as xenophobic, of proud to the extent of having little compassion for others. Sugihara, to be sure, is very Japanese, by any standard, but he also represents a more cosmopolitan tradition that developed around the turn of the century.

I traveled all over the world and found people who knew him through different walks of his life. His goodness seems to have left an indelible impression on them. I even discovered Sugihara's first wife, from a White Russian and antisemitic family, 93 years old and completely forgotten, in a Sydney old age home. She told me of their tender and very sad romance, under such dangerous circumstances. She hadn't seen him for over sixty years but still loved him dearly and could think only of his kindness to her.

Throughout this search which led me around the world and into some of its strangest places and most hidden archives, I found small clues which convinced me that Sugihara was a special man and that strengthened my resolve to discover exactly what was so special about him. He spoke many languages, an indication not only of his abundant talent but also of his strong desire to relate to others. His smile, as I discovered in a few photographs and as I heard from people who met him, was absolutely enchanting. I found a photograph of him standing outside the Kovno railroad station with some people who appeared to be rather ordinary. As it turns out, they include the head of the Polish Underground and his beautiful wife who Sugihara was helping to escape from certain death. Sugihara has such a relaxed look. I noted the cocky angle with which he wore his hat, his posture which exuded such self confidence, and most telling to me, the strength of the grasp of his umbrella. These small clues became so important in my interpretation of the man and his motives.

How baffled I was to discover his record in the Gestapo archives. His most private activities were reported upon in great detail. What there was no mention of was his most public act: saving the lives of thousands of Jews. Why was the Gestapo indifferent to what their man in Kovno was doing when he was not spying for them and what do we learn from this about so much more that could have been done to rescue Jews? As late as the summer of 1940—even later—Nazi policy was not necessarily to kill Jews. They wanted to get rid of Jews. Towards that goal they were eager and ready to use any means including murder. The Nazis who were spying on the Japanese spy had not special interest in reporting back about Sugihara's visa issuing activities. He was not only helping rescue Jews who otherwise were facing closed doors; he was helping his Nazi colleagues rid themselves of Jews. I am shocked to hear that there are historians who are now speaking of the myth of rescue. This Japanese representative of the pro-Nazi faction teaches us—of course we could have done so very much more.

I discovered Sugihara's own testimony about what he did in the summer of 1940. He says that he did what he did because of his love of life. I was rather disappointed. What a banal explanation for such a courageous rescue effort organized and executed with such cleverness. It seemed to me that there were far more profound ideas and deeper motives behind his mass rescue efforts. After resisting him but being unable to discount his own explanation for his actions, I came to realize that what he was saying was far more profound. So often we praise great people of heroism for their sacrifice and for their selflessness. We call this altruism. Sacrificial giving, at times is necessary and even noble. But there may be another type of motive for great acts that is no less noble and in the long run more reliable than this altruism which implies sacrifice.

Sugihara's emphasis upon the love of life, I am told, derives from his Buddhism which emphasizes this as a religious value. But it is difficult to establish what influence any religious ideas had on him. And it is equally clear that Buddhism as a faith has no monopoly on love of life as a spiritual value. Judaism also values love of life as an important incentive. In fact, this is well illustrated in the very statement in the ancient and sacred Jewish book of law and lore, the Talmud, ascribed to pikuah nefesh, rescue, and now made world famous by Steven Spielberg's Schindler. That statement, One who saves a single life, it is as if that person rescued the entire world, is, in fact, made in the context of a rather dry legal issue pertaining to the interrogation of witnesses in capital punishment. Rather than threatening witnesses with severe punishments in regard to the dangers of imprecise or false testimony, the Talmud suggest that we evoke within them this love of life. We remind them that saving a single life, is morally tantamount to rescuing the entire world.

This love of life, this affirmation of creation, creativity, and creaturliness has a power of its own. For a long while there was some reason for optimism. People of my generation were born while the ashes of Auschwitz were still warm and spent our formative years during the Cold War when for the first time, an increasing number of nations had the technical capacity to instantaneously blow up the entire planet. Nevertheless, we had some reason to believe that the horrors of the Holocaust, well known and accurately remembered, would draw the outer limits of what people could do to each other and inhibit future acts of genocide. In the world of the post-post Cold War, we are forced to recognize that the Holocaust may disinhibit, even model and legitimate acts of cruelty in a world in which we find ourselves with increasing capacity to remain impervious to genocide and deadly conflict. As we surrender that innocent optimism and struggle against the debilitating pessimism that comes from an honest confrontation with the human condition and an unflinching gaze upon the slaughterbench of history, the love of life might empower us in new ways.

In Sugihara, I discovered important lessons about the power of goodness. As our rabbis said, A good deed evokes another good deed and a bad deed evokes a bad deed. Sugihara's goodness was contagious. And it unleashed the goodness in so many other people. How else can we explain the fact that these Jews with Sugiharas visa of questionable value were able not only to enter the Soviet Union but to leave it, to be accepted by Japanese officials who were suspicious, to receive the kindest treatment from ordinary Japanese in the streets of Kobe and other cities? How can we explain this if not to believe in such things as—my fellow social scientists would revoke my credentials if they heard me speaking about this—of conspiracies of goodness?

In Search of Sugihara is an exercise in imagination, a fantasy about how the Holocaust could have been stopped, even at the very last minute. And what if there had been 10 Sugiharas, 100 Sugiharas, 1000 Sugiharas...? These are questions that we must ask ourselves.

NOTE

[1]Hillel Levine, *In Search of Sugihara* (New York: The Free Press, 1996), 197-99.

Never Let Complacency Guide Us Again

David A. Harris
Executive Director of The American Jewish Committee

"We cannot understand how you can eat and drink, how you can rest in your beds, how you can stroll in the streets—and I am sure that you are doing all those things—while this responsibility rests upon you. We have been crying out for months and you have done nothing."[1] Rabbi Weissmandel's desperate plea from Slovakia to Jewry in the free world in 1942 still haunts many people today. The question of what could have been done to rescue the European Jews from the Holocaust has been asked frequently. And it is among the Jewish community in the U.S. that this question still evokes emotions most.

Some concluded that the American Jewish leaders failed to mount a sustained or unified drive for government action because they did not have a strong desire to rescue Jews.[2] For example, Alan Dershowitz, a prominent Jewish lawyer, condemned the wartime Jewish leaders for they "totally misunderstood the pluralistic nature of American liberty and equality" when they "feared that by raising 'Jewish issues' in the midst of a great 'national' crisis, they might be pitting Jewish interests against American interests." For Dershowitz, rescue of the European Jews "would have been good for the Jews, good for America, and good for President Roosevelt."[3] Still others questioned, "Whether American Jewry, which amounted to only 3.6 percent of an indifferent public, among which anti-Semitism was widespread, could ever have exercised important political leverage in Washington—united or disunited."[4] One historian recently wrote, "While I would like to think that had I been an adult in the 1940s, I would have joined those activities pursuing rescue, my fear is that I would not have, that I would have been among those who found it easier to do less."[5]

It was with this question—reflection on the wartime Jewish leaders' stance and the lesson it has taught the post-war generation of Jewish leaders—that I met Mr. David A. Harris, Executive Director of the American Jewish Committee. AJC was founded in 1906 by a small group of influential Jews, including Jacob Schiff who volunteered to underwrite Japan's war bonds during the Russo-Japanese War, to defend the rights of Jews around the world. Together with the World Jewish Congress, it was one of the major Jewish organizations in the U.S. during the Holocaust. Although its membership was small, AJC "possessed substantial prestige and influence, had entry to some high levels of government and American society, and controlled considerable funds."[6] Yet, its leaders did not think their organization could exert a major influence on rescuing of the European Jews as its wartime executive vice president's remark revealed— "Nothing will stop the Nazis except their destruction."[7]

Today, AJC has 50,000 members. Its stated missions are "ensuring the security of Jews," "safeguarding pluralism" and "enriching American Jewish life."[8] Their activities also have expanded worldwide. For example, AJC spearheaded the successful drive in 1993 to establish a UN High Commissioner for Human Rights.[9]

Mr. Harris, together with Dr. Neil Sandberg, director of Asia and Pacific Rim Institute which AJC created in 1989, largely in response to the rise of anti-Semitic publications in Japan, visited Japan to promote a dialogue between the Japanese people and the Jews. They argued that "the lack of a strong government response to antisemitic publications were not in Japan's interests." The Japanese government, on their part, issued statements to the Japanese Publishers Association, informing them that antisemitic books were damaging Japan's international reputation." [10] Close observers noted that "the AJC's dignified, low-key, equable approach should serve as a model for future activism."[11]

Mr. Harris was named by *Lifestyles* magazine as one of 18 North American Jews who will serve as the leaders in the 21st century. He studied at the University of Pennsylvania, the London School of Economics and Oxford University. He has written three books and numerous articles on East-West relations and the Middle East.

I interviewed him at AJC's headquarters in New York.

What is your assessment of the level of knowledge about the history of the Holocaust held by general population? What are the lessons of the Holocaust we should learn?

People have the opportunity to learn about the Holocaust. Many of the school systems in this country and other countries discuss the Holocaust. There are any number of books, films, television programs, and now, of course, we in the United States have a very substantial museum. And also traveling exhibits, like that of Anne Frank. So I think the possibility for knowledge is there. But the challenge really is how to continually translate the meaning of the Holocaust as something that has significance and relevance for new generations of people, so it doesn't simply become another historical fact that people memorize. It should translate much more substantially than that. It should not just be a general awareness of what took place, but realization that civilized people stand between what took place and what might take place again somewhere in the world, whether against Jews or perhaps against other groups. So the real challenge is not just to get information out. The real challenge is to get information out and translate it in ways that have meaning and relevance, morally and ethically, for people today and in the future.

What do you think is the best way to achieve that?

I don't think there's any one best way. There have to be many different approaches. Perhaps in different societies and cultures different ways are needed. Lately, focus on individuals and the difference they made in the history of the Holocaust has become important. In Japan, for example, it is a focus on Sugihara, or on Schindler in Germany, or on Wallenberg in Sweden. I think this is very important because what it teaches us all is that an individual, you or I, can, if we choose, make a difference. This really destroys the argument that we are powerless in the face of evil. And I think that's a very important moral lesson. So, in that sense, a focus on individuals, individuals who try to act and, conversely, those who are complicit — or try to ignore—is important for us to understand.

To ignore means?

To bury their heads in the sand, to look the other way.

And they were the majority?

Yes, they were the majority, but what we learned is that individuals count. They can count positively; they can count negatively. But in a time of moral crisis, people cannot believe they can achieve some level of neutrality. Neutrality, by definition, becomes a kind of sub-conscious association with the oppressor. So, an emphasis on the difference an individual can make is one important approach.

But there is a danger even in this approach. The danger is that Japanese society, for example, begins to associate its history with Sugihara, or German society associates with Schindler, when in fact what Sugihara did ran contrary to his own Foreign Ministry, and what Schindler did was certainly the exception in Germany. So there is a danger here and we have to be conscious of it.

But I still think this approach of focusing on individuals and on the issue of ethics and morals—why certain people acted the way they did, what was in their upbringing, their family, their religion and their community that gave them the courage and determination to help—is important.

And they did not have to be saints or heroes did they?

Schindler was not a saint. Anyone who saw the movie realized that from the beginning. I think the most powerful thing about that movie was that he was a very unlikely hero. This was a flawed individual who could have been anyone, and yet there was something within him, some moral imperative, which led him to do what he did.

Now, that's a part of it. The second moral lesson of the Holocaust which we have to teach is that democracy is the single best form of assurance against tyranny and oppression. When Germany abandoned the democratic Weimar Republic in 1933, the safeguards and protections disappeared. The best form of government to protect human rights, civil rights and minority rights is a thriving, functioning democracy. It's not a perfect guarantee but still the best guarantee. But for a democracy to thrive and function, it requires the active involvement and participation of its citizens. And so the second lesson of the Holocaust, a practical lesson, it seems to me, is that good people have a profound stake in the system of government under which they live. It is true, we get the government we deserve, and, therefore, unless all of us care and act, we run the risk of governments that become anti-democratic, that become oppressive. So this is the second lesson of the Holocaust we have to teach.

You mentioned that people get the government they deserve. It is also said that people get the media they deserve. Of course, you remember the incident of the last year when one of the major Japanese publishing companies ran an article in their monthly magazine saying that gas chambers did not exist. I understand your organization's approach to that kind of incidents has always been that of educational, low key and behind the scenes. But it ended in an opposite manner. How do you feel about it?

I don't think there's any quick solution. Japan is a country of 120 million people and there are really no indigenous Japanese Jews. There are only 500 to 1000 Jews living in Japan, some of them for only a few years. So basically Japanese and Jews have very little contact and, even when they do, it may not be as Japanese and Jews but rather, say, as businessmen or professors. I think we have to understand that the challenge which we set for ourselves at the American Jewish Committee in 1987 in trying to develop relations between Japan and Jewish people is a long-term process. Those who wish to see immediate results will be frustrated. But there have been some encouraging developments. I have been especially pleased by the warming of relations between Japan and Israel. Israel brings not just political and economic, but also cultural and human, dimensions to the relations, and vice versa.

We are looking for more opportunities to introduce Japan to the Jewish experience. We have talked with some Japanese TV stations about the possibility of television programming. And although there are a number of books dealing with Jews, none of them is terribly popular in Japan other than the famous book of many years ago, *Japanese and Jews*. Maybe your book will be equally successful.

That was written by a Japanese author.

Yes. Again, there haven't been many popular books about Jewish people. Even the *Diary of Anne Frank*, which many Japanese proudly remind us is one of the best-selling books in the history of Japan, is not really seen as a Jewish experience by many Japanese. It is seen more as an experience of a young girl in a particular historical setting. It becomes a kind of universal metaphor for youth and suffering and dreams rather than a very direct expression of Jewish anguish during the Holocaust.

So there's still a lot of work to be done.

I am not one of those people who asserts that every Japanese is anti-Semitic. I don't believe that. I believe that there is much ignorance in Japan about Jews. There is some ignorance among Jews about Japan. I don't think the two are equivalent. There is much more ignorance in Japan about Jews, and it's very understandable. Jews are a very small percentage of the world's population. If we know more about Japan, it's because Japan has the world's second largest economy and is one of the world's major countries. When you have these incidents in the media from time to time, I think it embarrasses many responsible and educated Japanese. They know this is foolish and they know this is shameful, yet they also know that with a free press people can write what they want. But they know it stains the image of Japan. And it does, it really does.

Can I ask about your background?

I was born in 1949. I was the first person in my extended family to be born in the United States. Both of my parents came from Europe. They survived the war.

Survivors of the concentration camps?

They both had long and harrowing survival stories. My father, originally from Germany, had managed to escape from a special regime prisoner camp and spent the last two years of the war as an American espionage agent behind enemy lines in Yugoslavia and Austria. He came to the United States after the end of the war. My mother was born in the Soviet Union and later fled the communists, together with her family, to France. When France was occupied by the Nazis in 1940, she fled again, reaching the United States in November 1941. Every other member of my family had similar experiences.

So I grew up in a family here in New York whose members had been directly affected by the Holocaust in many ways. But I also grew up in a family which had been fighters. I really grew up with two aspects of the Holocaust. One was the reality of suffering and dislocation, of refugee experiences and hiding. The other, and this is more unusual among Jewish families in Europe, was that I grew up in a family that fought back—in the resistance movement, in the army. In a sense, without realizing it, both aspects became part of my own life experience. As a result, I came to feel I wanted to devote my professional career to participating in the rebuilding and restoring of the Jewish people after the devastation of the Holocaust.

Did you feel that way since a very early age?

No, sometime in my early twenties. First, I thought I was going to be a diplomat, but later I realized that I would rather work on behalf of the Jewish community and Jewish interests where I could focus my energies on the needs of the Jewish people. So, in a very real sense, the Holocaust has shaped my whole life even though I was born four years after it ended.

Did your parents talk about it when you were growing up?

Not very much. Like many survivors they didn't talk a lot about it. They came to America to establish new lives. But even though they didn't speak much about their experiences, it was in the air.

How did you feel about their experiences?

It is complicated when you're a child, because it's very difficult to filter all the things you hear. The first thing that struck me was that I was in a family where many different languages were spoken. You couldn't finish dinner without hearing three or four languages. And there were many references to many different places—for example, to Russia, Germany, Austria and France. This was my first taste.

The second taste was that our family members were scattered. I learned I had relatives in Israel, in the Soviet Union, in France, in Australia and, of course, in the U.S. We were a family scattered in five countries. Most families have relatives in the same country. Why, in my case, five countries? So I began to learn about these things.

My parents didn't hide things from me. But they didn't teach me every night about the history of the Holocaust, the need to remember, the need to be strong and all that, either. There was a kind of quiet dignity about my family. It was something I absorbed, I suppose, by breathing the air for so many years with my immediate family and with my extended family; it became very much a part of my own identity. As the time passed, I wanted not just to absorb it, but to see whether there was something I could do about it with the blessing of freedom I had been given, having been born in the United States.

I asked myself: Was there something I could do for the Jewish people rather than simply pursuing a career defined by making money or acquiring material goods? And, in the end, there was. I found it in my job in the Jewish community, which again was the direct result of the experiences of my family; all of that together created a foundation for my life. This happened slowly, though, almost unknowingly. And I now realize I was inexorably drawn into that direction and, by the time I was 25, it had become clear to me that this is what I wanted to do. I wanted to work in the Jewish community and on behalf of the Jewish people.

You chose a very old and established organization to do that, didn't you? I understand that the AJC is almost hundred years old and the people at the top must be much older than you. You are young. Why did you choose this organization?

The Prime Minister of Israel is younger than me, and his country is thousands of years old. Well, this organization, uniquely among the organizations I know, reflects the balance within me. It balances the concern for specifically Jewish interests and broader universal interests. This organization balances quiet diplomacy and public advocacy. In other words, this organization is quite sophisticated in its methodology and in the way it approaches issues. It also is a non-ideological organization. A lot of organizations, Jewish or non-Jewish, are ideologically driven. They are to the right or left, hawkish or dovish, conservative or liberal.

Your organization is not conservative?

No, we are not, not at all. We are a highly nuanced organization. That's who I am, too. Now, is it better or worse than any other organization? No, it's not a question of better or worse. Fortunately, the Jewish community has a range of organizations, like many other communities. This one matches me best. I want to be able to be concerned about manifestations of anti-Semitism in Japan, but I also want to participate in the broader trans-Pacific dialogue about relations between the United States and Asian countries. The American Jewish Committee is the only organization I know that allows me to do both.

It's not an organization driven solely by fear, not an organization simply protective and defensive. It's an organization that is protective and defensive when it needs to be. But, at the same time, it is also an organization that is forward-looking, believes in the possibility of a better world, and knows it can make a contribution to improving the world in which we live. Again, the balance between hope and fear.

Many agencies, Jewish or non-Jewish, are driven principally by fear. They believe that they can raise money and attract members by speaking to their fears. What we try to do is both to understand peoples' fears in the Jewish community, but also to speak to their aspirations and hopes. That's the balance I am most comfortable with. (I am speaking now in an American context and am not certain whether this is really understood in a country like Japan.)

But isn't there anything you would like to try that this organization did not do in the past?

This organization is 90 years old. I wasn't alive for the first 43 years of its history. This organization has enough achievements and accomplishments to fill volumes of books. And books have been written. It has a proud history of many years. It has a proud history of significant contributions to human rights and social justice and principles of fairness for all. I can go on and on.

Are there any moments in this organization's history that I wish could have been different or we could have rewritten? Yes. And the most obvious one is during the Holocaust period. I wish this organization, I wish Jewish organizations generally in the United States, had had the influence, the access and the ability to change the American policy towards Nazi genocide. And many people here to this day, 51 years later, continue to agonize over what might have been done differently.

Was there anything in our approach that somehow could have persuaded the American government to bomb the rail lines leading to the concentration camps, and thus slow down the extermination? And the answer here is that we almost certainly could not have changed the American policy, but we still should have tried even harder. Maybe we were too nervous, too worried about the possibility of unleashing American anti-Semitism as a reaction to our advocacy efforts. We weren't as self-confident in the 1940's about our place in America as we are 50 years later. Yes, I also inherited this legacy in my current job.

Now being in a leadership position, do you think about that past often?

I do. But I can't undo what has been done. I do not want to second guess because it is very easy to judge others with the perspective of the history. I would like to think that I know how I would have acted had I been in this position in 1941. But do I really know? Do I really understand the then prevailing circumstances, the configuration of power in this country, or the possibilities to influence decisions in this country, whether in the Congress or the White House or the State Department or the War Department? So, all I can do really is to try to learn the lessons of that history and seek to ensure that we are ever mindful of those lessons, that we are ever vigilant. We have to understand that we must never allow complacency to guide us.

We are supported by the Jewish community because they see us as a kind of radar system. They believe that an organization like ours needs to exist to keep an eye on what is going on; to understand when and how to act or react, how to address what remains the sense of vulnerability among many Jews because of the tragedies of Jewish history, including, but not limited to, the Holocaust. This sense of vulnerability is, by the way, often little understood among non-Jews who today see Jews as very powerful. They see Jews as very successful in America.

So do many Japanese. Some even believe that Jews are so powerful that they would take over the world someday.

Yes. Japanese see Jews as quite powerful. Some books in Japan go to great lengths to propound foolish conspiracy theories about Jews. Too many Japanese have no framework for understanding the sort of delicate psychology that exists. Of course, any people has a particular psychology, not just Jews. Japanese people are often said to have a superiority-inferiority complex. You have to understand the interrelationship between the superiority and the inferiority when you try to understand the Japanese. Well, among Jews, there's a different kind of psychology that you need to understand. That is the interrelationship between the external success of Jews and the ongoing internal sense of vulnerability of Jews.

So you must address the psychology of your people?

Yes. But there are many reactions one can take from the Holocaust. Some Jews say, for example, that there's no other historical experience identical to the Holocaust. They are right. I believe it was an entirely unique event. But what they draw from that conclusion is that no other events merit their attention quite the same way. The lesson I draw is that the Holocaust requires us Jews to be vigilant and take threats seriously, and not just against Jews. This is, if you will, a special moral obligation to be sensitive to other human rights situations, whether or not they amount to a Holocaust. For instance, we are very proud that the Japanese American Citizens League specially honored the American Jewish Committee for our considerable assistance, over many years, in securing reparations for the shameful chapter in American history of incarcerating Japanese Americans after Pearl Harbor.

I think that Jews, because of our experience of the Holocaust, have a particular moral responsibility, and, I might say, a special credibility to speak out against other tragedies, such as those in Cambodia, Bosnia and Rwanda, and we have. We have to talk about man's capacity for inhumanity, but also about the compelling need to try to bring greater sanity to this world. And it's no surprise that such a disproportionate number of Jews worldwide are involved in just such activities.

So you are optimistic?

I don't want to be pessimistic. I want to be realistically optimistic. I wish I could be unconditionally optimistic. But here we are, 51 years after the Holocaust, and we have seen brutal Communist repression, the Cambodian tragedy, and a horrible war in Bosnia. We see continuous strife and tragedies on the African continent, and we see intractable divisions in places like Kashmir, Cyprus and Northern Ireland. And anti-Semitism certainly hasn't disappeared, though it has fortunately diminished, for now at least. So it would be absolutely foolish and naive for me to sit here in 1996 and say that, 51 years after the Holocaust, however great the cost, however great the tragedy, people at least woke up and realized that unless they learn to live with each other, more human tragedies will take place, whether against Jews or against whomever. I wish I could say that.

But, at the same time, we today have democracy in more countries in the world than ever before. More countries respect human rights and civil rights now. I see these as very encouraging signs. And I see as well an international constituency made up of some governments, human rights organizations, individuals and groups like the American Jewish Committee that understand that unless they speak up, unless they act, unless they focus world attention on the problem areas, unless they remain persistent, there could well be regression. Unless they, we, have a moral backbone, the world will begin slipping back. But this constituency, I believe, is a strong constituency today.

People living in Latin America, with the exception of Cuba, would be the first to argue that there are indeed chances for improvement. Look at the remarkable democratic revolution on that continent. And people in the former Communist bloc would say, "Yes, it is a better world." True, economically they face real problems in making the transition. But there is genuine reason to be hopeful.

And the Jewish experience itself is perhaps among the best examples to suggest that one needs to cling to a certain optimism. Jews have survived every conceivable forms of hatred, oppression and tyranny; of organized systems of murder and extermination; of exiles, of ghettos, of pogroms. Whole new vocabularies were established to find ways to deal with Jews. And yet 3500 years later, not 35 years, not 350 years, but 3500 years later, here we are. Yes, here we are, a thriving people and a thriving State of Israel. And where are our oppressors? They are, in many cases, under ground. They are dead and buried, and many of their civilizations, too. From Hitler to Stalin and going all the way back. So the Jewish experience may be a very appropriate and encouraging metaphor for the power of hope.

But it's not hope alone. It's hope coupled with a profound commitment to a set of core values. And the values I am talking about, in addition to the power of faith, of course, are those of democracy, the rule of law, and justice, values consonant with Jewish ethical teachings and traditions.

"David is a very reserved person." Dr. Neil Sandberg told me before I interviewed Mr. Harris. During the interview, he himself said that he was most comfortable with the balance the American Jewish Committee seeks—the balance between quiet diplomacy and public advocacy. It was not easy at first to capture his personality aside from his public character as Executive Director of the American Jewish Committee. It was through the correspondence we exchanged after the interview that I came to know him as a warm and honest person. He wrote to me, "You asked important, probing and difficult questions…. I applaud your project and wish it well. Your goal of introducing Japanese readers to a range of Jews—and emphasizing our personal thoughts and life experiences—is a noble one that I hope will be well-received and have wide impact in Japan."

NOTES

[1]Michael R. Marrus, *The Holocaust in History* (New York: Penguin Books, 1987), 168.

[2]David S. Wyman, *The Abandonment of The Jews* (New York: Pantheon Books,1984), xi, 339.

[3]Alan M. Dershowitz, *Chutzpah* (New York: Touchstone, 1991), 294-95.

[4]Marrus, *The Holocaust in History,* 171.

[5]David Morrison, *Heroes, Antiheroes and The Holocaust* (New London: Milah Press, 1995), 325.

[6]Wyman, *The Abandonment of the Jews,* 67.

[7]Raoul Hilberg, *The Destruction of the European Jews* (New York: Holmes & Meier, 1985), 319.

[8]The American Jewish Committee, *Annual Report* (1994).

[9]The American Jewish Committee, *Making A Difference* (1996), 8.

[10]David Goodman and Miyazawa Masanori, *Jews in the Japanese Mind* (New York: The Free Press, 1995), 258-59, g.

[11]Ibid., 259.

Fighting Against the Holocaust Deniers

Rabbi Abraham Cooper
Associate Dean, The Simon Wiesenthal Center

"Do you know what the worst form of racism is? That is to say, 'What do you expect from the Japanese? They are different.' And there are people like that in this country. But I have seen so many things I like in Japan, met so many people I admire in Japan, and had so many special moments in Japan. I just have to find a way to communicate my concern."

Rabbi Abraham Cooper, the Associate Dean of the Simon Wiesenthal Center, a Los Angeles-based international human rights organization, was explaining to me why he had to protest against the *Marco Polo* article entitled "There Were No Nazi Gas Chambers" published by Bungei Shunju two years ago.

"For me, universal truths are as profoundly important as cultural differences. I've been to Japan many times. So I know we have differences between our two countries. But there are certain ethical standards which are universal and can breach cultural differences. To withhold comments because we are culturally different about what I consider to be universal issue of truth and responsibility wouldn't be my way.

I still remember that when we had an opening ceremony of our Holocaust exhibit in Tokyo City Hall in 1994,[1] I had a very moving conversation with a woman from Hiroshima. We had just cut the ribbon opening the exhibit. It was in that quite moving moment that I saw this elderly lady wearing a mask. She was standing in the back modestly and quietly. So at the first opportunity, I went over to her with my interpreter and spoke to her. I found out that she was an atomic-bomb survivor and came all the way from Hiroshima by train to show her solidarity with the victims of the Holocaust. I told her that I was very moved by her presence. With all of the other images at that day, thousands of people lining up outside to see the exhibit, important political figures including Ambassador Mondale, and many feelings and emotions, the most significant moment for me was meeting this lady. When I saw her standing in solidarity with us, I knew what I was doing was right and appropriate."

His eyes began to moisten as I was listening, spellbound. It was not his story, although his encounter with an atomic-bomb survivor was a beautiful one, but his ability to open up his heart and to allow himself to relate emotionally to another human being that I found to be remarkable. It must have required enormous courage and compassion for anyone who tried to talk to an atomic-bomb survivor and to relate to her suffering.

I could not help but wonder if anybody in the packed press conference in Tokyo really saw this person's compassion and humanity. Or did anybody really care to know what went through his mind when he said, "The *Marco Polo* article was akin to a denial of the dropping of the atomic bomb."?

Rabbi Cooper joined Rabbi Marvin Hier, the founder and the Dean of the Simon Wiesenthal Center, in 1977 to create an active Jewish organization in Los Angeles which would grow into a world-renowned human rights organization with nearly 400,000 members in a very short period of time. Its phenomenal success has often been attributed to the partnership between the two Rabbis : "Hier the often mercurial inspiration, Cooper the implementer who turned inspiration into action."[2]

Both are from New York and orthodox, the most religiously observant, Jews. Since the creation of the Simon Wiesenthal Center, Rabbi Cooper has been responsible for many of its successful international projects, traveling constantly to meet heads of states, influential politicians, human right activists and religious leaders around the world. His opinion on such issues as anti-Semitism, hate crimes, Holocaust denial and hate speech on the Internet appear regularly in major newspapers. Dr. Alfred Balitzer of Claremont McKenna College, an advisor to the Center who joined Rabbi Cooper's many trips to Japan, says that it is a combination of being savvy and sincere that makes Rabbi Cooper so successful in dealing with media.[3]

Rabbi Cooper is no stranger to the Holocaust deniers. Wiesenthal Center World Report, *Response*, of which he is the editor-in-chief, has exposed many Holocaust deniers around the world and their activities. As early as 1982, Rabbi Cooper protested against a high school teacher in Los Angeles who was teaching his students that "the 6million Jews killed by the Nazis" was an exaggeration. Rabbi Cooper's stance was clear and simple. He wrote, "…while we all must insure freedom of expression in our society, we also have a responsibility to guard historical process and truth."[4] Over the years he has spoken out on this issue many times whether the denier was the Syrian Defense Minister, a professor in France, a key PLO leader, or a well-funded neo-Nazi organization. Since most of the "charges" made by these deniers were identical, the Wiesenthal Center published *Holocaust Denial,* a handbook listing deniers around the world and providing point-by-point refutation to their "charges."[5]

In the mid-80s, Rabbi Cooper became concerned about the explosion of anti-Semitic books in Japan. He visited Japan many times to find out how and why these books were so popular. He visited all the major book stores in Tokyo and found out some stores even set up a "Jewish corner." According to Dr. Balitzer, however, it was also through these trips, that Rabbi Cooper learned the nature of "Japanese anti-Semitism" which was very different from that he had seen elsewhere. Dr. Balitzer remembers the moment when Rabbi Cooper was surprised to see such anti-Semitic books placed right next to *Diary of a Young Girl* at one bookstore in Tokyo.

After returning from one of these fact-finding trips, he urged Rabbi Hier to write a letter to then Prime Minister Yasuhiro Nakasone requesting that he "publicly condemn these books, which constitute an unwarranted attack on the Jewish people and represent a disgrace to Japanese society."[6] Yet, anti-Semitic books continued to sell in Japan. In 1988, Rabbi Cooper wrote in the *Japan Times* that the popularity of such books would have an adverse effect on Japan's image.[7] Also in 1993, when Nihon Keizai Shimbun ran an ad for a three-volume series of books alleging a Jewish plot to destroy Japan, he immediately protested while the Los Angeles Times supported his action by writing in its editorial, "Civilization will never advance until we stop perpetuating racial, ethnic, religious or gender stereotyping and scapegoating."[8]

The Marco Polo incident occurred in spite of these efforts by Rabbi Cooper in the previous 10 years. When the Simon Wiesenthal Center learned about the article, he immediately sent a letter of protest to Japanese Ambassador Shoichi Kuriyama. Also, a request to withdraw future advertisements, together with the article itself, was sent to several international companies which had placed their ads in *Macro Polo*. Upon seeing this development, Bungei Shunju sent its U.S. bureau chief to the Simon Wiesenthal Center to meet with Rabbi Cooper and to express their regret. It later sent an official apology admitting that they had lacked an understanding of the historical facts and that their article had caused immeasurable pain to the Holocaust survivors and the Jewish community. The letter also notified the Center that Bungei Shunju would recall all the copies of *Marco Polo* carrying the article from bookstores, relieve the responsible staff members, and close down the magazine. The Simon Wiesenthal Center accepted the apology praising the Bungei Shunju's immediate and unprecedented action.[9]

These developments were explained a few days later at a news conference in Tokyo by Bungei Shunju's president, the U.S. bureau chief and Rabbi Cooper representing the Center.

Later, the Simon Wiesenthal Center conducted a three-day seminar on the Holocaust for employees of Bungei Shunju. Rabbi Cooper was one of the lecturers. Executives of Bungei Shunju also visited Center's Museum of Tolerance in Los Angeles.

I remember vividly when I first met Rabbi Cooper. In early 1996, I was organizing a tour of the Museum of Tolerance for members of the Japan America Society of Southern California and hoping to have a memorable reception for the participants. I decided to ask for support from Rabbi Cooper.

The Simon Wiesenthal Center, compared with its impressive Museum of Tolerance next door, is housed in a rather humble building. I was waiting for Rabbi Cooper in the lobby, imagining what kind of a person he would be. From the newspaper articles I had read at the time of *Marco Polo* incident, somehow I had an impression that he was an old religious figure. Then, a very energetic and much younger person that I had not expected ran down the stairs. "So, this is Rabbi Cooper...," I said to myself with pleasant surprise.

In his room, I explained my plan for the reception. He promised his support saying, "An action is always better than an idea." Not only did he support my plan but also he himself attended the reception and greeted more than 70 Japanese people on the day of the tour.

A few months later I decided to turn another idea of mine—writing a book about those who devote themselves to making the world remember the Holocaust and the lessons it has taught—into an action.

I interviewed him in his office where a Japanese language poster of "The Courage to Remember" was prominently displayed on the wall.

What was your first concern when you read the Marco Polo article?

How it would hurt the Holocaust survivors, especially because it came out at the 50th anniversary of the liberation of Auschwitz. I don't know if there is a similar tradition in Japan, but we call it "Yahrtzeit" in Yiddish. It is the anniversary of the death of loved ones. Every year you light a candle in memory of your loved ones. I light a candle in spring time once a year for my father who passed away eleven years ago. And all the memories come back. I am sure it's universal. So, the notion that for anyone in a position of power and responsibility to introduce such a hurtful idea during this time—that is not an action which I, as a human being and as a Jew, certainly someone who carries the name of Simon Wiesenthal, would allow to stand.

Was that the reason you called for a boycott?

An economic boycott would have meant a much larger scale action, like writing a letter to Fortune 500 companies and all of the advertisers of *Marco Polo*, and actually stating publicly that we were calling for a boycott, which we never did. We selected a half dozen or so international advertisers and basically asked if they knew what was going on. The article was an absolute outrage. But, even in that outrage there was never an attempt to say, "Let's investigate *Marco Polo*" or "How do we destroy *Marco Polo*?" Not at all. What we wanted to do was to make sure that the international addresses who were underwriting *Marco Polo* advertisements understood that something went terribly wrong—crossing the line from legitimate journalistic inquiry to hate propaganda.

Also, the Simon Wiesenthal Center never demanded that Marco Polo be shut down. What we did request was to educate people at that publication, sitting down together and going over in detail what it was that deeply and profoundly upset us.

Why did you go to Japan and have a press conference there?

As I told you, my first priority was the victims. Always. I had to make a gesture on behalf of their pain. I think the victims of the Holocaust need to be protected. They have already suffered enough. But they are not historians, they unfortunately went through the event. So what the society, good people, and caring people can do is to express their solidarity with the victims and to help them feel that they are now more protected and more loved.

At the same time, there's also a relationship with long-range concerns, long-range hopes and goals. So I wanted to explain to the Japanese people why such a serious step was taken. If it wasn't for money, and if it wasn't to destroy a company, and if it wasn't because it despised Japan, then why the Simon Wiesenthal Center did it. We did it because we believed that there are universal ethical standards—standards that can and should be applied to even powerful media companies.

So you were happy with the way it turned out?

We appreciated the opportunity to present a seminar on the Holocaust for the Bungei Shunju's employees. But the damage was already done. We have to understand as we are entering the world of the Internet, that article is now a part of history, available through the Internet to the main stream culture. It will appear again and again in different formats all over the world in Japanese and in other languages. It was a victory for professional Holocaust deniers whose goal is to spread prejudice and hatred against the Jewish people.

*Indeed, the Institute for Historical Review, a California based organiza-
tion posted in its home page that a major Japanese monthly magazine
had presented credible evidence to show that there were no execution gas
chambers in wartime German concentration camps.*

Yes. We are very concerned about the spread of violent and racist
materials on the Internet. Last year we sent a letter to hundreds
of Internet access providers in the U.S. asking to adopt voluntary
guidelines that would terminate services to individuals or groups
promoting such materials. Also, we set up our own home page
(http://www.wiesenthal.com) to present accurate information
regarding the Holocaust.

*Some in the Japanese media seemed to have taken your action as an
infringement on their right for freedom of speech. What has been your
position on this issue including this incident?*

A basic approach for the major democracies or for human rights
organizations like ours is that we have to start with the understanding that you cannot legislate hate out of the person. In our
society, there is no constituency for government-installed cen-
sorship. Americans like the idea of maximizing speech. So they
have a "right" to say anything and even to submit a whole page
ad presenting the same thing *Marco Polo* article said. But, the
New York Times won't accept such an ad not because there is a
governmental rule, but because this great newspaper sets its own
standards. Therefore, if you live in a democracy and are in a powerful position, you have a great opportunity and a responsibility.
Exercise them. Exercise critical thinking, especially when you are
in the media as a gate keeper of ideas in a democratic society.

A while ago, Holocaust deniers tried to publish their ads in
college newspapers, and we responded by writing a letter to every single college newspaper in America. We told the students
that we were not afraid of the idea in the ad because the Nazi
Holocaust was the most documented human rights violation in
the history of mankind. So it's not the issue of "proving." Our
suggestion was not to tear up the ad but to tear up the check and
turn the fact of this advertising campaign into a newspaper story.
Expose this phenomenon of Holocaust denial. Call in Holocaust
survivors and experts to inform and educate other students. That,

to me, is Freedom of Speech. Accepting the check and ad because it's an easy thing to do and to say that's freedom of expression, I consider it to be a cop-out. If I had an opportunity to discuss it with Japanese journalists and academics, I would have liked to talk about these basic issues. Perhaps in the future.

Professor Deborah Lipstadt who wrote Denying the Holocaust: Growing Assault on Truth and Memory, *which was translated into Japanese recently, refused to engage in a debate with the deniers, because she believed that to do so would give them a legitimacy and a stature that they in no way deserve.[10] Did you refuse to write a response to the Marco Polo article for the same reason?*

Yes. So called "charges" of these deniers are relatively easy to refute. But the essential thing for us is not to elevate their bigotry as if there were a legitimate "alternative view" to the reality of the WWII Nazi Holocaust. Remember that *Marco Polo* was a monthly magazine. That means there could be no immediate response. And the magazine's editorial lead to the article was an endorsement of the article. It's like a major American magazine carrying a cover story saying the whole Hirosihma thing was a fraud and the all of the people suffering from the sickness caused by the bomb were lying. Next month, those who suffered were invited to answer. Would that satisfy people in Japan? I don't think so.

How would you respond to an opinion by a prominent Japanese journalist who wrote, "So this whole thing meant a reaffirmation of existence of the taboo that we could not touch."

Contrary. That brilliant person missed the entire point. I might not have explained well enough at the press conference what it was that we were most concerned about. I am not afraid of liars. I am not afraid of racists. But in order to combat them, you have to be able to put them in an appropriate category. There are no issues that are taboo. It is appropriate that 10 and 50 years later to visit and revisit historical places and issues, including the Holocaust. New documents may come out that would enable us to better understand the event. That is an appropriate definition of revisionism—a term now 'hijacked' by extremists.

Let me emphasize again that if there are people or groups devoting themselves to rewriting history or denying history, the public has a right to know about these groups and they should hear their argument. Actually, I would welcome a series of articles or maybe a TV program presenting the phenomenon of Holocaust denial and analyzing why it's taking place and what financial and political forces are behind it. But again, they should not be presented as alternative views with the mantle of legitimacy, that have the same footing as the brutal reality of the Nazi genocide.

If you want to talk about real taboos in Japan, then you would do well to look at the questions of Japanese behaviors during the Second World War and the years before on the Asian continent. You see, these perpetrators, the victims, the survivors of Hiroshima and Nagasaki—that generation is leaving the world scene very shortly. Now is an appropriate time for the younger generation to get the lessons from the people who survived these horrific events. It's the last opportunity for the generations to reach out to each other. But, it seems unlikely that those who committed atrocities during that period will break the silence. And the forces of truth and reconciliation are damaged whenever statements are made by Japanese officials, like for example, "The Nanjing massacre never took place." For too many people in Japan, those kinds of issues remain taboo in 1997. The good news is that's not true for all Japanese whether it is the issue of the "comfort women" and the other very painful issues. We all need to fully confront the past before we can make demands on future generations. I have three children. How can we expect young people to make moral and ethical decisions if adults are not dealing with their shortcomings.

Your long time friend Dr. Balitzer said that you were a man in action with a deep commitment to justice and an abundance of energy. What motivates you? What is the driving force?

I came from the generation born right after the Holocaust. We had a lot of anger about what happened to our preceding generation. You had a teacher who had no extended family, you had a friend with no grandparents, and you had a neighbor screaming at night with a nightmare. And you just wanted to say out of frustration to your own elders, "I am sorry, but you didn't do enough. Something should and could have been done. History should have been different." So the next logical step for us was, "Change! Make a change. Participate. Do something." Remember, it was also the time of Martin Luther King Jr., the possibility of all kinds of change through a non-violence movement.

When I was in high school, I was involved in a movement called "Student Struggle for Soviet Jewry." It was a non-violent movement like letter writing campaigns, demonstrations at the United Nations, and eventually a trip to the Soviet Union at the age of 22. In those days, many Jewish leaders said to our generation that public protests would make the situation worse for the Jews in the Soviet Union. They might be correct. But we would say, "Wait a second, what happened to the Jews who kept quiet when Hitler came to power? We live in a democracy. We have to find a way to change the reality."

Well, I'd like to believe I am a bit wiser now, I know I am much older. But the feelings from those days still affect my life everyday and impact on the way I act.

Another aspect of the driving force is the inspiration I found later from Mr. Wiesenthal. He always spoke since the first time I met him of the need, the opportunities and the responsibility of building new bridges between peoples.

I notice that you have never talked about your fear. Do you have a moment that you fear that a tragedy like the Holocaust will happen again to the Jewish people?

I have a faith that says that Jewish people are an eternal people and that we will outlast our enemies. I know that there are many racists, bigots, hate groups, and people who don't like Jews even though they never met a Jew in their life. But the opposite is also true. There are many people who show their solidarity The main thing is never to fear. God keeps saying, "Fear no one but me." That, on many days, is easier said than done. But when you have access to a living legend like Simon Wiesenthal and everything he and his generation went through, we really don't have a right to complain very much.

After 12 years of trying to build bridges between the Japanese people and the Jewish people, what is your feeling toward Japan now?

I believe that the bilateral relation between the U.S. and Japan, as well as that of Israel and the U.S. is going to be very important for many decades to come. They will also continue to be very complicated relations. To add a more personal note about why this remains important to me, I would say that I am very much attracted to Japan. There is a saying in Hebrew, the ethic of one of our great teachers two thousand year ago, that says, "Who is a wise person, he is prepared to learn from everyone he meets." There is so much to admire in Japan and I am still learning.

Additionally, I don't think we have a moral right to speak out and protest unless we are ready to also engage in a dialogue. It is easy to stand far afield and to say when an incident happens, "Oh, those Japanese," or "Isn't that terrible?" I am not interested in that. I have a firm unalterable belief that there are universal truths, but I also realize that just because these universal truths exist it doesn't necessarily mean that they are going to compute unless we are willing to translate them and grapple with them on a human level. In this connection, I am particularly interested in having dialogue with young people in Japan.

Finally, history itself plays a role. I often think about the difference between trips to Europe and trips to Japan. when I get off from the plane in Europe in almost every country, there are reminders of the terrible history of Jewish persecution in the last two thousand years. The very problematic blood-soaked Jewish history. When I get off the plane in Japan, that baggage doesn't exist. It's a different slate. It means that maybe there can be opportunities to establish new relationships. When I was a student at Yeshiva University in New York, I had teachers who had been in Shanghai during the war, some of them went through Kobe, and spoke of small but positive contact with Japanese people. The same government that made a decision about Nanjing also allowed 25,000 Jewish people to survive the war in Shanghai. The Holocaust was such an incredibly dark chapter in terms of European history and Christian values that I don't think the Japanese people should be shocked that there were Jewish people looking to see if there were other cultures where a sprout of friendship and mutual understanding would come up.

But as it happened, most of what Jews read about Japanese and what Japanese read about Jews in the past 25 years has been, to say the least, controversial. It is the hope of the Wiesenthal Center to help take this relationship to a new level. It's going to take the involvement of many many people, many groups, and influence of the government. But we have to start from somewhere. And I consider it to be a privilege to be a part of that process.

There is a small room on the second floor of the Museum of Tolerance where visitors can listen to testimonies of Holocaust survivors. Exchanges between the survivor and the listeners, especially young people, are always moving. After a testimony some hug the survivor and say, "Thank you for having survived and telling your story for us."

One day, I was specially touched by a testimony of a beautiful Auschwitz survivor. I went over to her and asked if she had been speaking about her experience for a long time. She answered, "Yes, for almost 20 years. Rabbi Cooper started an outreach program for us to go to local high schools and to share our experiences with students. At first I was not sure if young people would be interested in my experience. But Rabbi Cooper insisted that this was very important. So here I am, after 20 years, it became my career." I imagined young Rabbi Cooper accompanying this beautiful survivor, being his mother's age, to high schools so young people could learn about the Holocaust. I also remembered that he once told me that being with Holocaust survivors was a more humbling experience than meeting with kings or politicians or any other people.

Some people, both Japanese and Jewish, told me that the way Rabbi Cooper had handled the *Marco Polo* incident might have enforced the stereotype that the Jews were powerful people who controlled the world. But the Rabbi Cooper I came to know was much more concerned about reaching out to Japanese people at a personal level than just creating a favorable image of Jewish people. He told me that he used to sit down on a bench in a Japanese park on weekends and watch family outings. It was at such a moment, he said, that he realized that there were universal truths in humanity that we could learn and relearn from each other.

Whenever I meet Rabbi Cooper I am always struck by his being devoid of cynicism. I will always remember what he said to me at the end of our long conversation. "As long as there is a moment like the meeting with that lady from Hiroshima, I believe what I am doing is worthwhile."

NOTES

[1]"The Courage to Remember" (Exhibit) at Tokyo City Hall, May 10-20, 1994.

[2]Yaron Svoray and Nick Taylor, *In Hitler's Shadow* (New York: Nan A. Talese, 1994), 29.

[3]Interview with Dr. Alfred Balitzer, February 22, 1997, Long Beach.

[4] The Simon Wiesenthal Center, *Response*, July, 1982.

[5]Sol Littman ed., *Holocaust Denial: Bigotry in The Guise of Scholarship* (A Simon Wiesenthal Center Report 1994.)

[6] The Simon Wiesenthal Center, *Response*, September, 1987.

[7]Abraham Cooper, "Japanese Anti-Semitism: A Mystery, Absurdity and Threat to Japan's Image," *Japan Times*, June 28, 1988.

[8]"Blaming It All on Them," *Los Angeles Times*, August 2, 1993.

[9]"To Our Readers—About Our Decision to Close Down *Marco Polo*," *Bungei Shunju*, April issue, March, 1995.

[10]Deborah Lipstadt, *Denying the Holocaust: The Growing Assault on Truth and Memory* (New York: A Plume Book, 1994), 1.

In Memory of One and A Half Million Jewish Children

Rev. Makoto Otsuka
Director of the Holocaust Education Center in Japan

One and a half million—that many children perished in the Holocaust. Why did so many children have to die? How could the people of Germany, one of the most cultured nations of the world, believe that killing these children would constitute "a page of glory in their history"?[1] These are the most difficult questions for us to face in the history of the Holocaust. We learned that children were always among the first to be sent to the gas chamber at Auschwitz. With the death of those children we lost one and a half million futures and possibilities. Elie Wiesel, who lost his beloved sister at Auschwitz, gave the saddest reason for the killing of so many children. He wrote, "Why were they the first? Somehow it was as if the killers and the children couldn't co-exist under the same sky.[2]

The children who perished in the Holocaust left us not only with a profound sorrow but also with some of the most moving episodes during that tragic time. The story of Janusz Korczak, a renowned Polish educator who ran an orphanage in the Warsaw ghetto, and his students was one of them. He "used all his connections, energy, and ability to help his orphans survive in dignity, to feed them, clothe them, sustain and educate them.[3] On August 6, 1942, the Nazis struck against the children's institutions in the ghetto…. Korczak stood at the head of his wards, a child holding each hand…. There were none of the cries and screams usually heard when people were forced to board the trains…. One witness recalls: 'This was no march to the train cars, but rather a mute protest against the murderous regime…a process the like of which no human eyes had ever witnessed.' Korczak was with his children to the end. All were gassed at Treblinka."[4]

We see today drawings and poems by children of the Terezin concentration camp because of the efforts by Friedl Dicker-Brandeis, an art teacher who encouraged the children to express themselves even under the unbearable living conditions. Of those 15,000 children who passed through the Terezin less than 100 survived. *I Never Saw Another Butterfly,* the collection of poems and drawings by these children, is published throughout the world today.

The Holocaust Education Center located in Fukuyama city in Hiroshima prefecture, Japan was opened in July of 1995 for the purpose of commemorating one and a half million children who perished in the Holocaust, and teaching the Japanese Children the importance of building a future without discrimination and prejudice. The Center is supported by the "Japan Christian friends of Israel" and is open to the public.

On the outside wall of the Center's building is the star of David with the Hebrew word for "Life" inside. At the entrance, visitors see a special message from Elie Wiesel to the children of Japan:

Dear Children,

As one who has devoted his life to the cause of remembrance, I urge you to enter this hall with open heart.

What you will see here will cause you fear and pain. You will ask yourselves: how could all this happened? Why have so-called civilized people decided to assassinate an entire people? How did they manage to kill thousands upon thousands of Jewish children and remain sane?

If there is an answer, it is in memory.

With best, best wishes,
Elie Wiesel

Dr. Michael Berenbaum, who was the Project Director of the United States Holocaust Memorial Museum called this center "a little jewel" when he visited here in 1996. Almost twenty thousand people have visited the Center since its opening, most of them school children. On the exhibition are items donated from Holocaust survivors and related institutions around the world, such as a little shoe worn by a child who perished in the gas chamber. The exhibit is designed in such a way that little children can see items and read explanation easily.

I first learned about this Center from those whom I interviewed in the United States. More than once I was asked, "Do you know your own country has now a Holocaust Museum?" They also told me about Rev. Otsuka, Director of the Center. I was pleasantly surprised to know that after spending almost a year interviewing people who devote themselves to teaching about the Holocaust, there was someone in my home country who is doing exactly that.

Rev. Otsuka welcomed me when I visited the Holocaust Education Center from Los Angeles. Our conversation lasted for hours. I felt as if I were talking with a long time friend while he explained to me how he got involved in creating the first Holocaust institution in Japan and in what direction he would want to bring the Center.

Could you tell me about your first encounter with the Holocaust?

> It started with my meeting with Mr. Otto Frank, father of Anne Frank, 26 years ago. He lost his entire family in the Holocaust, but he seemed to have overcome the tragedy and believe in the future. He told me, "Don't just grieve over the death of my daughter, but do something to make the world a safer place. Peace can be achieved only through mutual understanding." Those words of his left a lasting impression on me. Later, I had an opportunity to visit him in his home in Bazel, Switzerland and saw him writing a letter to all these children around the world from whom he had received a letter. I remember telling myself that this, caring little people, indeed was "peace education." I decided at that moment that I should do what Mr. Frank was doing.

During the 25 years that followed your meeting Mr. Frank, what led you to finally creating this Holocaust Education Center?

As I learned more about the history of the Holocaust and became aquatinted with some survivors, I could not help but ask
myself, "why did these decent and innocent people have to go
thorough such an unspeakable tragedy?" I am still trying to find
an answer to that question. It happened in the most enlightened
society in Europe. We had Ms. Hanna Pick, who was a close
friend of Anne Frank visiting us when we opened our center. She
was 68 years old, younger than our parents' generation. Had Anne
lived, she would have been still that young. Then you may realize
how recently the Holocaust happened.

It is said that the majority of those who attended the Wansee
Conference, where the "Final Solution to the Jewish problems"
was discussed, held a doctoral degree. I came to think that the
Holocaust happened as the culmination of people's tendency with
which they judge people on the basis of religion and race. Then I
realized that this tragedy challenged us, not just Nazis and the
Jewish people but all of us including Japanese, forcing us to grapple
with this fundamental issue for human beings.

I also realized how dangerous it is to have a society whose
majority did not care about the fate of the minority. Except for a
very few courageous people, nobody tried to stop the mass kill-
ings of the Jews. People simply did not see Jewish people as their
fellow human beings. Don't we have "lack of sympathy for less
fortunate," "self-centered attitude," and "prejudice for different
people" in Japanese society today? Is our educational system trying to address these issue as forcefully as they can?

At the same time, I learned that survivors and Holocaust educators were committed not only to remembering this tragedy but
also to educating people, especially young people, to make the
better and safer future. I decided to do the same for children in
Japan.

I wrote letters to survivors and Holocaust-related institutions
around the world asking to send me any items that could help
Japanese children learn about the history of the Holocaust. I was
astonished when I found myself receiving almost 2,000 items
from all over the world. This Center became possible because of
these gifts and support from those who sent them.

*I saw them on display. A prison uniform worn by an inmate, utensils, a
brick from crematorium, and a tiny shoe worn by a child who perished in
the gas chamber.... I was particularly touched by the many photographs*

of children during those days. How did you feel when you received these items?

> I was overwhelmed by the outpouring of their support and kindness. Every item I received was attached by a letter thanking me for using it for the education of Japanese children about the Holocaust. I think these items are treasures coming out of tremendous sufferings. I also felt an enormous responsibility of becoming a custodian for these artifacts. I renewed my commitment that I would do my very best to utilize these precious gifts so that Japanese children can learn important lessons from the Holocaust.

I saw a several letters from survivors directly addressed Japanese children. Every time I listen to a survivor talking to young people, I was always moved by their genuine love and affection for the children. Perhaps it has something to with the fact that most survivors went through the Holocaust as a young adult. I see the same affection in the letters displayed in this Center.

> My hope for the future is in you, the young people. I hope and trust you will be taught tolerance for each other, so that you shall be able to live in harmony with your fellow men.
>
> Valerie Furth, a survivor of Bergen-Belsen

How have you been trying to convey the message from survivors to Japanese children and what have been their responses?

> I always talk to children very passionately. Without seeing any note, I look them in their eyes, and talk as if each encounter with children is the only chance I am given. I am aware that many Holocaust educators suggest that we should wait teaching this subject until children reach at least junior high school age. But I believe I can teach much younger children here. I would say to elementary school students, "there were many children just like you who were victims in this tragedy."
>   I will never forget a remark by one third-grader when I was talking to a group of elementary school students. I showed an

artwork done by a Holocaust survivor, which depicted a mother whose child was about to be executed. I asked students how they felt and this third-grader answered, "I wish I could take his place for her." Then the whole group clapped their hands. These children knew nothing about Hitler or Nazis, but they did have compassion for this mother who was about to lose her child. It was at that moment that I knew what I was trying to do was right. I wanted to teach these children about fundamental values in human lives. The teachers who were there still talk about their being deeply moved by this exchange.

That must be a very special experience for children, too.

Yes. I think Japanese children today are not being educated in such a way that they can learn lessons for their lives. They are taught to memorize subject matter. I think they are yearning for the real lessons that can guide them throughout their lives. But for teachers and parents to provide children with such education, I believe that they themselves have to learn the real lessons in life. Because we can only teach what we ourselves have learned.

What has been people's response to this center in the last two years?

Almost everyday, children visit this center with their teachers. Thanks to the media coverage the center received, visitors are coming not only from the local areas but also from far away places. Those who have visited this center have told us that what we were trying to do here was a wonderful education. When the opening of this center was announced, the Consulate General of Germany in Kobe told us that they were concerned if there were anti-German message in our exhibit. So, I invited them to the center so they could see for themselves. After the tour of the center, they said that this was a remarkable educational center.

I always think that I myself am learning with visitors. Although we don't charge an admission fee, this center is not conveniently located so people can stop by after shopping. People spend money to travel to get here. I tell myself all the time that if these visitors don't learn valuable lessons worth their travel, that would be my failure.

We also have visitors from foreign countries, such as the United States and Israel. We issue an English newsletter and set up a web page on the Internet (http:/www.urban.or.jp/home/hecjpn/)

I heard that many prominent people have also visited here.

Yes. In July of 1996, on the occasion of our first anniversary, Dr. Michael Berenbaum, the former director of Research Institute of the United States Holocaust Museum visited us and gave a speech entitled *Children of the Holocaust.* We also had President of Hebrew University in Israel visit us.

And you attended an international seminar on Holocaust education.

Yes. I attended a conference held in Jerusalem in October of 1996. More than 300 people, museum staffs, educators, scholars and guides, gathered there. I myself did a thirty minute presentation using video tapes describing activities at our center. Since I was the only participant from Asia, people were interested in what we were doing in Japan, and I was interviewed by many reporters from various countries.

After the conference I visited Eastern European countries where I could speak with many survivors of the Holocaust. Attending that conference and traveling places where the Holocaust took place made me determined more than ever that we must educate young people in Japan about this tragedy and the lessons it left.

This is something I have been feeling. But don't you think that the Holocaust is a topic which makes it possible for those who are working on it to develop a deep sense of friendship among them? Given the enormity of this tragedy, I find this to be very profound.

I feel that way, too. I think it is because the Holocaust was a tragedy created by people. In a way it started in the mind of people. That is why those who try to prevent another Holocaust from happening again care about human relations so much.

I was surprised and moved to encounter again in this center the same pictures I saw at the Holocaust Memorial Museum in Washington D.C. It was a collection of pictures depicting the peaceful lives of residents of Ejszyszki, a Jewish Lithuanian town which was destroyed in just two days by the German mobile killing squads in 1941. Rev. Otsuka told me that Professor Yaffa Eliach of Brooklyn College, who was one of the only few survivors of that massacre and who spent many years collecting these pictures, sent 70 pictures from her collection to this center. With those pictures on the wall was her message to Japanese children:

> Dear children of Japan:
>
> On behalf of all of the children of Ejszyszki, who were among the million and a half Jewish children to perish during the Holocaust, I would like to wish you, the children of Japan, a different kind of future. May you grow up in a world without hate and war, and may you live long enough to fulfill your dreams.
>
> Your friend,
> Yaffa Eliach

NOTES

[1] Speech by Heinrich Himmler at Poznan on October 4, 1943, quoted in Martin Gilbert, *The Holocaust* (New York: Henry Holt and Company, 1985), 615.

[2] Elie Wiesel and John Cardinal O'connor, *A Journey of Faith* (New York: Donald I. Fine, Inc. 1990), 64.

[3] Michael Berenbaum, *The World Must Know* (New York: Little, Brown and Company, 1993), 78.

[4] Ibid., 80.

Coping With Our Own Brokenness Can Make Us Humane

John K. Roth
Professor of Philosophy, Claremont McKenna College

I decided to see Professor John Roth because of a beautiful essay he wrote. That essay, entitled "Elie Wiesel's Challenge to Christianity," appeared in *Elie Wiesel: Between Memory and Hope*, a collection of essays by eminent scholars on the issues in Elie Wiesel's work. There, Professor Roth remembered his encounter with the Holocaust that forever changed his life. He wrote:

> My reading of Elie Wiesel began in July 1972, just a few days after my second child was born. My wife and I named her Sarah. In more ways than one, my entry into Sarah's world coincided with my entry into Elie Wiesel's. For in the latter I would meet another Sarah.... Tensions created by the contrast between my joy as Sarah's father and the despair of "Sarah's world" portrayed...by Wiesel in his novel *The Accident*—these were among the catalysts that ever since have compelled me to respond to his words in writing of my own.
>
> The first essay I published in that vein was called "Tears and Elie Wiesel." It began with a reflection: "Lately something has been puzzling me. I do not regard myself as an emotional person, so why do I sometimes find myself about to weep? Nobody notices, but why is it that especially in church on Sunday mornings tears well up in my eyes?" This experience has continued; it is one reason why I still go to church. In writing that initial article more than fifteen years ago, I began to understand that my tears were partly a response to Elie Wiesel's challenge to Christianity.[1]

Professor Roth, the son of a Presbyterian minister and father of new-born Sarah, had to respond to the challenge presented by the world of Elie Wiesel's Sarah, who, at the age of twelve, had been sent to a special barracks for the concentration camp officers' pleasure. He went on to write:

> Christianity was not a sufficient condition for the Holocaust, but it was a necessary one. Remove Christianity and Sarah's world would not have been. That is a specific, concrete way to encapsulate Elie Wiesel's challenge to Christianity. The challenge, however, is not just about the past. It involves judgment about the present and the future as well...[2]

So began the journey of Professor Roth. A prominent Holocaust scholar, he has published more than twenty books and hundreds of articles. He recently reflected, "...my writing has explored themes such as Jewish-Christian relationships; the theological implications of the Holocaust, especially as they affect Christianity; the challenges that the Holocaust poses for philosophy and for ethics in particular; and America's encounters with the Holocaust."[3] From the very beginning of his encounter with the Holocaust, the question of Jewish-Christian relationships seems to have occupied a major part of his academic and personal inquiry. For example, in *Approaches to Auschwitz*, which he co-authored with Professor Richard L. Rubenstein in 1987, he wrote:

> When first confronted with the horror of Auschwitz, one may ask: how could it happen? Historical research reveals how and, to a large extent, why the Final Solution *did* happen. The story is millennia long. In special ways, religion marks it indelibly, bringing the makings of catastrophe. Those ingredients lodge in tensions between two groups, one spawned from the other, who have seen themselves as God's chosen people.[4]

If the Holocaust could be seen as the culminating offspring of religiously inspired anti-Semitism, what lesson has Professor Roth, a devoted Christian, learned from studying it? Is there any universal aspect in his search that has a relevance to largely non-religious Japanese society?

These questions kept coming back as I read some of his writings. Yet, it was the essay I first read that left a lasting impression on me. I simply wanted to see the person who was so utterly honest about his feeling in encountering the history of the Holocaust and the responsibility of his own religion for it.

I met Professor John Roth in his office at Claremont McKenna College where he has been a professor of philosophy for the last 30 years. The school year had just ended the previous week, so the campus was quiet when I visited his office. Having expected to meet a person in his 50's who had been grappling with the darkest topic imaginable, I was surprised by his boyish look. Also, there was something in him which immediately made me feel comfortable talking with him. So I started.

Have you found an answer to the challenge that you wrote about long time ago?

> No, I don't think so. I think Elie Wiesel's perspective on the Holocaust is the right one. It leaves us with many more questions than it does with answers. I think the purpose of studying the Holocaust, teaching about it, building museums and encouraging people to learn about it is not to make everybody an expert on the history. I think there is a moral purpose so that we become more sensitive and better able to relate to other people in the way that makes life good rather than destructive.

It seems to me that your emphasis on the importance of human interaction is, if not an answer, at least a major lesson you have drawn from the history of the Holocaust. You wrote about "the fatal interdependence of all human actions," a phrase by Gitta Sereny who interviewed Franz Stangl and his wife after the war. Franz Stangl was the commandant of Treblinka where more than 800,000 Jewish victims were murdered. Asked by Sereny which her husband would have chosen if he had been forced to choose—Treblinka or his wife—Stangl's wife answered that her husband would in the final analysis have chosen her. Stangl himself said that if he had refused his orders it would have made no difference. It would have gone on just the same.[5] Yet you wrote that if more individuals had done for each other what was very much within their power to do, to call each other into account for their actions, the Holocaust need not have gone on just the same.[6] Could you elaborate on that?

Yes. When I read Sereny's book, that phrase, "the fatal interdependence of all human actions," stuck in my mind. My own philosophy about human actions and human life is that they are interconnected very strongly. I think I learned some of this by living in Japan for a while. In 1981 and 1982 I was a visiting professor at Doshisha University in Kyoto. I was very struck when I was in Japan that the Japanese society has much deeper sensitivity and appreciation about relationships than in the United States where we talk so much about individualism, self-reliance and independence. My own philosophy is informed by the conviction that things are related and that a person is understandable only in terms of social ties that he or she has with other people. So whatever we do, I think, we affect other people just as we are affected by what other people do. That means, then, that there can be a chance for people to make a difference and to affect other people. I think as a teacher I experience this to some extent all the time. It's fragile. You can't absolutely control what happens because these relationships are complicated. But a person is responsible not only for what he or she does but to some extent for other people, too. I think this was a point Sereny was wanting to bring out in her study of Franz Stangl. There is this web of responsibility, and we have to be responsible for each other. One of the things this means is that we have a better chance of acting the way we should when we are in a community where people support each other well.

But being a member of a community doesn't mean that a person makes a right decision, does it? Community as a whole can go in the wrong direction.

Yes, you are right. Of course when you look at what happened in Nazi Germany a lot of people were supporting each other to do wrong. But if you flip the coin, one of the things that appears in literature and testimonies of people during the Nazi years is that there would have been more dissent and more resistance if people had felt there was greater support for them. So the lesson I take from this is that it often is very difficult to do what is good and right if you are absolutely alone.

I thought that the group orientation of Japanese society was our weakness when it comes to individual decision to do right things since we tend to discount the individual's capacity to make a difference.

Well, I often thought that if there could be a blending of the best part of Japanese society and the best part of American society, this would be a goal to aim for. You are right that Americans have an individualistic streak about them that can often make Americans rebellious, defiant, protesting and taking stands. That can be good, especially if the resistance and protest are for a right cause. And we had examples of that in our history. That would be one of the safeguards against a social mentality that might be very strong but headed in a direction that is destructive. On the other hand, we haven't taken relationship or community so seriously for some time and our society has suffered for it through violence, crime, and disrespect for other people. So, if there can be a blending of the communal support that Japanese society has so strongly with occasional infusions of individualism that might come from sound moral perspectives, I think it would be a good mix.

Can that infusion come from something other than religion?

Oh, sure. My own view about American life, or human life for that matter, is that concerns about what is good and what is not can come from a lot of different places. I think the basic concerns that people have for what is good and what is not tend to have a lot in common from one culture to another. So my view is that you want to draw on any and every resource that you can find to support those things. Religion is something that can do that. It doesn't always do so—religion has a dark side, too. It can be intolerant, destructive and even disrespectful of human life. But when it's at its best, religion can be something that helps to create a community with a sense of common goodness and a sense of respect for individual life. As a philosopher who is interested in morality and ethics, I will take whatever I can find to get the support.

If it's not religion, what did you find in Japan that you thought gave Japanese people such moral support?

One thing is that philosophically, or I use the term "spiritually" here, Japan is a place that draws on varying traditions and blends them together in an interesting way. But what I learned from Japan came more from living there and observing the people. I may be idealizing, but there was a positive disposition or attitude about people working together, helping one another, and serving one another. That was impressive to me. You see it in an everyday way that a person living in Japan might just take for granted. For example, there is a certain kind of orderliness in the way in which people relate to each other and the way in which people are ready to help one another. Americans do this, too. But there was something about the feeling of it in Japan that was interesting to me. It's hard to put into words. It's courtesy, civility and respect that go with the importance of working together to have the group succeed. Individuals take satisfaction and pride from that as opposed to the view that says "I am going to get what is out there for me. I don't really care what happens to the other people." That was the part that I thought Americans could learn more about. It could strengthen our society.

But didn't you see a danger? In a society like Japan's, don't people tend to follow whatever is considered to be proper by the group rather than to follow their own conscience? If children are taught only to follow the rules of the society, can they make their individual decisions when they have to?

Well, I think it takes both because each individual's conscience is nurtured by his or her parents, schools, community and society. My appreciation for the things that I am describing in Japanese life comes about, to a considerable degree, because of what I think is lacking in my own American society. And this ties into the concern about the Holocaust. I am worried about American life because we may not cope well with the fact that our population is getting bigger and more diverse in the 21st century. Diversity is something that we prize, but it also is something that can create tension, difficulty and distrust that can lead to violence. So, the big challenge we have in American society is how we are going to live together.

You also have to be very careful about the seductiveness of certain ideas that build senses of community that are false and

destructive. In Nazi Germany this involved a kind of national-
ism that was predicated on racism. This idea rested on an ideology about the inherent superiority of one group of people over
another. The Nazis carried very intense prejudice and hatred
against certain groups that were looked upon as threats. Now
you can build a kind of community spirit out of these elements
because some people want to feel that they are part of the "in"
group. And to make that feeling strong it helps to have enemies
that you can point to and say, "These are bad people and they are
against us." But we have seen that if the spirit of community is
resting on these foundations, then the consequences are deadly.
So the problem is hard. In order to have a life that is really good,
we have to have a community of some kind. I am convinced of
that. Then the question is how do you shape the community so
that it is healthy and able to handle diversity.

How can learning from history play a role in shaping such an ideal com-
munity? Have you read a recent LA Times *article about the Japanese*
debate on how to teach history, especially its dark chapters, to young gen-
erations?

Yes. I was specially interested in that article because I just came
back from a conference held in Northern Ireland where I was
invited to talk about what happened to women during the Holocaust. But people there included two women, one Korean and
one Dutch, who had been so-called "comfort women" during
the war. They told about their experiences. And after I got home
I found the *Los Angeles Times* article that was essentially a revi-
sionist view.

The article was about a group of people in Japan who argue that if teach-
ing of history places too much emphasis on the dark side of nation's his-
tory, such as the rape of Nanjing or the comfort women, then the young
generation won't feel proud of their nation and that kind of education is
not healthy.

My feeling is that you have to face the truth. If you don't face the
truth, then you are living a deceived life and that's going to have
bad consequences. But there are different ways to face the truth.
There are ways that can embitter people and make people feel

guilty in a way that can be very counterproductive. So, the way in which the truth is taught and handled becomes important because what you want to have happen is that people take responsibility for the past but are not driven into defensiveness or some other reaction to the truth that inflicts pain and suffering on other people all over again.

How can we do that? I kind of gathered that you felt some collective guilt for what happened in the Holocaust as a Christian. Should it be that way for Japanese people?

I think I can speak from my own experience here. When I began to learn more and more about what happened in the Holocaust, my own identity began to come into question for me because of the Christian background that I have. I have to think about what it means to be a Christian in the time after the Holocaust. My identity as a Christian is something that is valuable and meaningful to me, and it's something that I don't wish to flee from or give up. But as I learned more, I thought about the question of what it means to have an identity as a Christian, or I would even say as an American or as a professor after the Holocaust. I often suggest to my students when we study the Holocaust that no one comes away from it without being affected in some way. Professors and teachers in Germany, for example, were part of the process of destroying the Jews of Europe. American identity also comes into question because of the history that reveals what Americans did or didn't do during the Holocaust. The reactions I had ranged all the way from anger against what others had done to my tradition, in the sense that I was not old enough to have a direct responsibility for what happened during 1930's and 1940's since I was born in 1940. But I think that what I feel more is a combination of shame and responsibility. Shame, not because of anything particular that I did during this time, but because I am a part of the Christian tradition that was involved, implicated and responsible because of the anti-Jewish parts of Christian history. What I conclude that I can do is to take responsibility for my tradition and try to do what I can to keep it from making the same mistakes again and perhaps to make, in some small way, a contribution to redeeming or restoring the credibility of that tradition. So, that's a challenge and, in a way, it has had the affect of deepening and intensifying my own religious outlook.

So, your encounter with the Holocaust didn't shatter your faith?

No, at least not entirely. The study of the Holocaust for a person like myself always cuts in two ways. One part of it makes you uncertain and unconfident. And you find your life dealing with questions all the time. Another part makes you know what you ought to try to do and what you ought to try to be in a way that is intense. It doesn't mean that you'll succeed, but at least I think you are clear about what's right and what's not, after you study about the Holocaust for a while.

What made you think in that positive direction instead of thinking, "So, my religion and tradition were not so great after all."? That reaction is what some Japanese educators are arguing would happen to the young people if we teach them negative aspects of our history?

I can be critical of both my national tradition and my religious tradition. And in order to be true to both of those, I think that I have to be critical. But I can't reject either of them because they are so much part of who I am and they are, in addition, a large part of what I regard as good about my own life. If I have been able to do anything as a professor, as a parent, and as a son, it's all mixed up with the religious tradition that is mine and also with the fact that I am an American. So, I can't reject these things or I would, in a way, destroy myself. What I can do is to be critical of the things that deserve to be criticized and, at the same time, I can try to support and enhance the things that are good in these traditions. I think this is something important about traditions in general. Tradition is something that you aren't just handed or you aren't just given. You have to make it your own. There's a way to do that well, and there's a way to do that badly. The way you do it well, I think, involves critical sifting, sorting and deciding what's good and what isn't, and how you could move in the direction of enhancing what's good.

In most cases in human history, if you plunge deeply into it you will find a mixture of good things and things that aren't. But if you immerse yourself in it you will also find that there are strands and veins of goodness that you can identify with and that can nourish you at the same time. Take part of the Holocaust as an example. On the whole, you can say that the record of Christian conduct during this time was not anything like it should have been. But if you study the history you can find examples of Christian behavior that are as noble and as worthwhile as anything you can hope to find. I am thinking here of people who helped to rescue Jews, who risked their own lives, and who took stands. These are a very small minority of the total population but they are the ones who reveal a standard to aim at, probably a standard that most of us can't reach or can't achieve. But they are the ones who show us what ought to have been the case in a way that is not just theoretical or hypothetical, but that was embodied in the lives of these men and women who acted that way. And I think the same thing is true for one's national tradition. In study of the history of a nation, you can see plenty of things that deserve criticism. I remember my visit to Hiroshima with my son. It was an unforgettable experience for me which involved feelings of anger and shame. I know there are all kinds of arguments made back and forth about how necessary the atomic bombing was. But when you go to the place and see the destruction and walk on the ground as an American, it is very hard to feel proud or even to feel patriotic, because what you recognize is so much suffering and destruction. It's overwhelming.

On the other hand, I can see in my own country's history a lot of other things that are good and worthwhile. One's task as a citizen is to honor what's good and to try to sift and sort out as much as you can what isn't. It always ends up as a mixture.

Are you comfortable about not being certain about certain things?

Yes, I am. This is partly because of my training as a philosopher. I think human life is better off when people aren't too sure about things. Mischief and destructiveness break out most often when people are too sure, especially when they are sure that they are right and therefore that other people are wrong.

Does one have to be a philosopher to accept that uncertainty?

Oh, I hope not, although I think human beings tend to prefer certainty and answers more than they do living in ambiguity and with questions. But on the whole, I think people can live with a mixture that is something like this: we aren't absolutely sure that what we believe is true but we still have enough confidence about what's right and what's wrong so that we can take action and not be paralyzed by doubt and uncertainty. This is something I learned from Elie Wiesel. He has always been very supportive of people who have other traditions than his as long as they are honest and as long as they are really trying their best to be true to the best parts of their own tradition.

Assuming there is the best part in each tradition?

Yes. Now, we don't want to say that Nazism had a best part. But if you took German culture before it got so deeply imbedded in anti-Semitism and Nazism, we can certainly find many things in it that we all value. So if your identity is German, then I think the task for a German after the Holocaust is to do what you can to redeem German culture and German history.

There is another insight. There is a saying in Jewish tradition that goes something like this: There is no heart that is as whole as one that has been broken. It's a paradox. What it means is that when your heart is broken, you feel and respond to the fact that your life is less than it could have been. And that sensitivity can become the first step toward healing. How we cope with our own brokenness is maybe where the differences between being humane and being destructive lie.

Are you still crying in church?

Yes, sometimes. If I were to sum it up in words, that experience involves, on the one hand, a deep feeling for how good, beautiful and moving human life can be, and, on the other, how much human beings do to waste life, destroy it and disrespect it. And sometimes it seems like those negative features are prevailing more than the ones that try to encourage people to honor and respect life. When tears come, it happens very quietly. It's subtle. But sometimes I do find tears in my eyes. They can appear in unexpected times and places. Sometimes hearing some lines from the Bible can do it. Sometimes the sound of music can produce them. Sometimes the feeling I have inside can come from reading a paper that a student has written, where I can see that the student has been touched by something he or she read in the Holocaust course that I teach. It can come by seeing images that are photographic or in film. I never quite know when the experience will come, but I welcome it because I think that feeling can teach me important things.

You have to be careful about feeling, though. Emotion is explosive and volatile. It can carry us off in all kinds of different directions, some of which can be very dangerous and destructive. So feeling and emotion have to be balanced with critical thinking. But there are points at which emotions are good teachers for us.

Are you satisfied with the way that you took up the challenge you first faced 25 years ago?

An encounter with the Holocaust is bound to leave all of us unsatisfied. But what you will experience and discover as you follow where the Holocaust's questions will take you is valuable and instructive in a historical, ethical and spiritual way.

Do you think you are a different person now?

Oh, yes. I am more melancholy and sad than I am used to be, although I still have a sense of humor. My immersion in the Holocaust's history has helped me to cope with my own small degree of personal adversity in a way that makes me grateful. If I ask myself what is the most important thing that I do in my own work, I think it's clearly teaching about the Holocaust, trying to think about it and write about it, and trying to make some contribution to prevent destructive human conduct.

Where is your Sarah now?

She is in Seattle doing public policy analysis.

Holocaust: Religious & Philosophical Implications, which Professor Roth co-edited with Dr. Michael Berenbaum, former director of the United States Holocaust Research Institute of the United States Holocaust Museum, was dedicated to their students. The dedication says, "To Our Students Who Have the Courage To Go into That Darkness and Beyond Against Despair."[7] I read that book many times, including his own essay entitled "On Losing Trust in the World." But I had never considered myself a student in the study of the Holocaust until I met him. Or more precisely, until I saw a picture we took together. The afternoon when we took that picture was so beautiful and so peaceful—a campus without students, vines on the wall, gentle sunbeams, and the bicycle that Professor Roth told me he rode to his office everyday...

When I looked at the picture of us standing in that beautiful afternoon I found myself being emotional. I could not explain my feeling for a moment. Then I remembered what he told me at the end of the interview, "What still brings tears to my eyes is my recognition of how good, beautiful and moving human life can be on one hand, and how much human beings do to waste it, destroy it, and disrespect it on the other." I realized that I had become his student on that day.

NOTES

[1]John K. Roth, "Elie Wiesel's Challenge to Christianity," in *Elie Wiesel: Between Memory and Hope,* ed. Carol Rittner, R.S.M. (New York: New York University Press, 1990), 78.

[2]*Ibid.,* 80.

[3]John K. Roth, "It Started with Tears," in *From the Unthinkable to the Unavoidable: American Christian and Jewish Scholars Encounter the Holocaust* ed. Carol Rittner and John K. Roth (Westport CT: Praeger Publishers, 1997), 195.

[4]Richard L. Rubenstein and John K. Roth, *Approaches to Auschwitz* (Atlanta: John Knox Press, 1987), 8.

[5]*Ibid.,* 361.

[6]*Ibid.,* 362.

[7]John K. Roth and Michael Berenbaum, eds. *Holocaust: Religious and Philosophical Implications* (New York: Paragon House, 1989), v.